VUKULU SIZWE MAPHINDANI

I'm Still A
Kaffir

SECOND ANNIVERSARY EDITION

CLASSIC AGE PUBLISHING

I'M STILL A KAFFIR

First Published by Classic Age Publishing in 2018

Private bag x134

Braamfontein Johannesburg 2001

www.classicagepublishing.com

Book Cover Design by Louis Gibson

Editing by Fahamu Jami

Typesetting by Classic Age Publishing

ISBN: 978-0-9947069-6-6

Table of Contents

Preface

This book is not for everyone. It's written for those who are interested in race relations and who, for many reasons, acknowledge the reality of black people's denigration in South Africa, the rest of the African continent and globally. It is also for those who are conscious of present-day's mass incarceration of black people since PW Botha's Total Onslaught of 1978. Botha's Totalitarian strategy waged war scientifically, Socially,

Economically, and medically against black people. And even after 1994, during Nelson Mandela's turner as president — The inequality gap between Whites and Blacks had become appalling than anywhere else in the world. So given such circumstances, especially in a country that considers itself a democracy with the best constitution in the world, a conversation on contemporary state of affairs is 911.

As a result of the former, I found it very necessary to write a thought-provoking material that will likely spark a critically unique debate about the South African State of affairs. And as much as the title may be deemed controversial, at times, it's necessary to employ confrontational language in addressing our frustrations as a race of people that is Native to the

South African land as much as we are native to all civilizations in the world after all that we have gone through for the past four hundred years in the hands of Whites. There is no one black person out there who can confess that they are slaves/Kaffirs, just like there is no one mad person who can accept that they are mentally defective. Therefore, I believe that the only way to defeat this spiritual behemoth of dehumanization and inferiority in global black communities is for us to become loyal and committed towards Blackness because we have for several years promulgated a short-sighted and a fractured thought process towards self, and we need to relook at our black racial personality against the conflagration of racial inferiority. So, my determination is a critical imposter of self-determination on blacks' epistemic survival as we continue to reform our Black Humanity by rescuing self from the consistent thrust of White psychological abuse just like in all aspects of people's activity — Economic, social, political, scientific, Nutritional, technological, etc. All my writings are written out of the undying love I have for the Black race!

Acknowledgements

I find it almost impossible to write this section of the book because if I have to truthfully acknowledge the people who have been around me during my spiritual journey through Black Consciousness, I would be writing two full books at no fail. But I will try my best to grapple with inserts of what still secures space in my memory bank. First, I genuinely believe that if it was not for the following warrior ancestors, we could have been spiritually castigated and exterminated a long time ago. But they ensured that our spiritual epistemic and cultural nature of our self-preservation could not be compromised.

TIYO SOGA (1829 – August 12, 1871) - I first learned about the elder in the person of Tiyo Soga from the book titled Biko A Biography by Xolela Mangcu [2012]. When reading the book, I was more interested in learning about Steve Biko's philosophical nitty-gritty on his conspicuous Black consciousness ideology. Although, amidst my realization that iconic figures such as Tiyo Soga were some of the earliest intellectuals to give rise to the Black Consciousness philosophy, the eclipse of the philosophy thrived during the time of Steve Biko. Even though he was a Christian evangelist, Tiyo Soga was one of the earliest Black Intellectuals in South Africa. He is the first Blackman in South Africa to write a journal, and his views encouraged internationalism regarding Africans' common destiny – both at home and abroad. One hundred and thirty-one years later, his contributions to Black intellectual thought is not permeated from widening our scope of intellectual engagement. To this ancestor, I pay my very first homage.

SOL PLAATJIE (October 9, 1876 – June 19, 1932) – I first learned about elder, Sol Plaatjie as early as 2003 when I was reading about the formation of the South African Native National Congress that was later renamed the African National Congress (I don't recall the publication well). At first, I knew about Sol Plaatjie as

only one of the founders of the African
National Congress until I came across a
book titled Native Life in South Africa by
Sol Plaatjie [1915]. Sol Plaatjie's
intellectual scholarship and prolific
writings usurped my determination
towards writing and progressive activism.
I became an author and publisher because
the insurrectionism of Sol Plaatjie's story
neutralized my thinking, which could
have been destroyed by White
psychological abuse through mind
conditioning with instruments such as the
education and media in South Africa. I
also was very fond of Plaatjie as I am
today because we were both born in
October. I wanted to become Sol Plaatjie
just like I wanted to become a Marcus
Garvey or a Malcolm X.

Anton Lembede [January 21, 1914 – July

30, 1947] – I first learned about the concept Black Inferiority Complex When reading some writings documented in the Library of Giyani (South Africa) back in 2004 written by Anton Lembede. He is, following most journals and South African History publications, profiled as the Founder of the African National Congress Youth League, which was and is still arguably completely different in ideology with the African National Congress. Anton Lembede is the original architect of the concept of African Nationalism in South Africa. Unfortunately, when African Nationalists left the ANC to form the Pan African Congress in 1959, the elder had already passed away much earlier than that. To this ancestor, I pay my third homage.

As indicated, if I were to credit

every contributor to my spiritual journey, I would be writing two full books. I take note of the contributions of all freedom fighters, those who have been executed by the Colonial and Apartheid government in South Africa. Those who were hanged, those who were incarcerated without trial, those whose contributions are still to be discovered, etc. The likes of Steven Bantu Biko, Solomon Mahlangu, Lilian Ngoyi, Winnie Mandela, Robert sobukwe, John Dube, and everyone else I couldn't mention.

In 2017, I founded the Black Centric Forum Movement in South Africa, a post-liberation Black Consciousness and Black Nationalist organization together with my beloved sister, Valerie Montja. In essence, I henceforth, send special regards to my warrior sister. I also send special considerations to brothers and sisters like Itumeleng Makale, Thapelo Lairi, Tebogo Seichoko, Nontokozo Ngema, Thato Thenda, Salosh baka, phumza Nciweni, Nokwanda, Ntsiki Mazwai (my co-founder of The Black Imbizo Platform) and all brothers and sisters within the leadership of Black Centric Forum, so is the entire collective family and chapters of the Movement.

Last but not least, I cannot consider myself sincere enough if I can leave out my two beautiful children; Rhandzu and Tupac Maphindani. Their transitioning to this universe has shaped me spiritually in ways I cannot explain; I, therefore, send my special regards and love to them for being born from my loins. To my father, Winston Maphindani, and my mother, Josephine Maphindani — in me, you gave birth to a warrior, and thank you for raising me with love, support, and truth. And to my three brothers, Mponisi, Muhluri, and Johannes – let's keep the family together and carry on the struggle for our family's spiritual, social, and economic destiny.

INTRODUCTION

'm Still a Kaffir is exactly what you think it is – a 911 critical assessment of the Black condition by myself; a Black consciousness adherent and warrior, whom, through lived experiences shares a South African inspired perspective on the subject matter herein with direct reflections from my own life. This is a letter disguised as a book. Besides being a letter, I have written a memo to indoctrinated black masses whose fate is plagued in an era of psychological remote control and ecocide (Economic Genocide). Consider this letter a symbolic gesture in response to the psychologically disguised neo-colonial exploitation in the form of debt, menticide, divide and conquer, ecocide, Trends, Social Media, biological weapons (AIDS, Ebola, Swine Flu, cancer, listeriosis, Corona, etc.), nutric-ide (nutritional genocide), Music, war on drugs, police brutality, blacklist, black inferiority complex, prison industrial complex, Video games, internet, and mis-education. It is proven beyond time and memory, neutralized by further study and research, that the inherent and shady symbiosis between blacks and whites draws most of its inspiration from Charles Darwin's views on *The Origin of species.*

In merely some dopey theory of evolution, he argues that "Blacks are monkeys" (Indirectly but very purposeful). And although detractors may argue in denial that he indirectly presented "blacks as monkeys," the theory of evolution is graphically illustrated, and the message is unambiguous.

As in many written texts justifying the inferiority of black people, whites have been consistent in maintaining this grandiose behavior. Because it's necessary for their unfounded ego to justify the enslavement of black people, because even today – Whites in South Africa still hold the conviction that Colonialism civilized "black savages" and that Apartheid was never a crime against Humanity, with the recent of the series of commentary coming from the former and very last Apartheid president of south Africa – FW "Idiot" De Klerk. Such a Cosmological rubric of Apartheid and colonialism denialism in South Africa is very dangerous because it carries in it a multigenerational transmission of a false conviction and belief in White Supremacy - a very ideological and historical non-starter unless Whites are only willing to listen to the language of violence for them to repent and commit to reparations in South Africa. The word "Kaffir" as a keyword in this discussion was borrowed from the Arabic language, and it translates to a "non-believer" in English. So by giving a historical context of that word here in South Africa; It referenced a people who were systematically engineered to become projects, objects, subjects and natural resources in the building of White Power - and those people are none either than black people whom for over three hundred and forty-two years, have been murdered, raped, dehumanized, kidnapped, brainwashed, incarcerated and repeatedly oppressed simply because they welcomed visitors who masqueraded as allies knowingly that they were a bunch of criminals. Given such a disturbing account of violence, three hundred and sixty-six years later — that exploitation and systematic abuse have resurfaced economically under the guise of the Private Sector (Institutional racism and the industrial monopoly complex).

Chapter 1

I'm Still A Kaffir

'm Vukulu Sizwe Maphindani, a Black warrior and a king in his own right – a descendant of Nghotsa, a great warrior of the North in today's Limpopo Province. I was born at Mninginisi Block 2, a small village in Limpopo, South Africa. As a young Black who lived most of my life under the system of democracy although born during the Apartheid era, this book relates my spiritual testimony regarding my position as a "Kaffir" in this White-terror-domination or cluster called South Africa because it is problematic for me to denote myself African today (Considering the great and rich African history) whilst I carry the burden of subordination.

I'm the fourth son (last born) of Saina and Risimati Maphindani. My parents got married in 1976. My mother, the firstborn of Thomas and Ndaheni Maluleke, is a former slave of the Oosthuizen family. Her story with that family dates back to the 1960s (when she was a teenager) in a farm located in Soekmekaar, which, by that time, produced tea bags and coffee beans from cultivation, nurturing, and harvesting. It was only in 2001 when she opened up about her experiences with me, as I have begun critically assessing the history of South Africa, Apartheid and Colonialism. As much as her experiences were seemingly disturbing, she took it lightly and even joked about that – but those confessions have given me sleepless nights and goosebumps ever since, and served as the most significant contributor to my determination towards the politics of reparatory justice in South Africa.

I believe that my mother's story made more sense when narrated in Tsonga, for which is the language we use at home anyway. *"A hi tirha mahala ku sukela hi matakuxa kuyafika avupela dyambu"* which translates "we worked from sunset till sundown without pay," she asserted. She was, alongside her fellow slaves, beaten from morning to night by extremely tough and gigantic Afrikaner males who never bothered much about their "Black teenage slaves" but their selfish economic gain through slave labour. Her Afrikaner bosses or slave masters would be wandering around the farm smoking Cigars, on their "Khakhi shorts" (The Boer's signatory attire) and those who happened to take naps or breaks before sundown, they would immensely be beaten and forced back to the post regardless of the bodily harm experienced during the attack. There was no lunch nor drinking water and no resting during working hours. As she continued to tell me about the events on the farm, it took me time, and a few years to consume that problematic part of my mother's history. I even thought that she could have also been raped consistently, but how can a mother explicate such a traumatic experience to her own son about 40 years later. But as much as when explaining the many horrible scenes on the farm, she was bubbly; there was something critically depressing about her tone of voice.

I began to read more about the history of Apartheid, colonialism, slavery, Jim crow, plantations, mass incarcerations, gas tanks, and the oppression of black people after my mother's Apartheid story, I then realized how much bad the Black state is. And if exercising what you call a comparative narrative – I came to learn that slavery in the United States of America and Apartheid/colonialism South Africa was no different. It was the two sides of the same coin.

The difference between plantations during slavery in the USA and Farms during Apartheid in South Africa

When studying the history of slavery and Jim crow in The United States of America. I came to learn that when Africans were kidnapped against their will, in most West African states and throughout the continent of Africa. I realized that the history surrounding the events was not so isolated to the entire global black existence. The very first people to enslave Africans were the Romans, in what was called Chattel Slavery between 533 to 695 AD. After the Romans, we were then enslaved by the Arabs and, lastly – The Europeans.

In what is today called the transatlantic Slave trade, where over thirteen million Africans were seized, over two million of the captured Africans/slaves died in the middle passage. Some jumped to the ocean; others died of famine, others due to slave raids upon arrival, and so forth, and so on – such a human tragedy is very frustrating to talk about. These groups of European Mafias who operated the slave trade were mainly from Britain, Portugal, Netherlands, France, etc. When slaves were sold to the slave masters or those who bought the slaves – their names (slaves), culture, spirituality, and practices were stripped from them and as a property belonging to the slave master – they were forced to take his religion, his language, his name, his surname, his heritage and way of life. This was compulsory, and the slaves who resisted were either publicly murdered in front of other slaves, auctioned, or publicly humiliated. The slave master's house and farmstead were relatively coined, "The Plantation." A plantation was a place where slaves owned by a specific cracker/slave master lived and worked for free. They were working under horrible conditions, in most farms, they would be picking cotton and other agriculturally related activities based on what the slave master's economic activity was. They worked from morning to night without pay and were allowed to pray on Sundays and to sing "Negro spirituals." Their slave masters, instead of calling them dispossessed Africans, identified them as Negroes or Non-believers. In the plantations, wives were separated from their husbands; the male master would rape a mother, her daughter, and her son because some masters were pedophiles. At times, for slavemasters who were homosexuals, they would rape the Blackman or father in front of his wife and children and, at times, kill him. This very experience repeatedly happened for about 300 years, even though Abraham Lincoln had signed the emancipation proclamation in the year 1863. Hundred years after the emancipation proclamation was signed into law, in 1964, President Lyndon Johnson passed the Civil Rights Act in 1964 subsequent to constant resistant groups like the Civil Rights Movement of Dr. Martin Luther King and others who kept on pressurizing the American government to abolish discriminatory laws like Jim crow and others in the USA. As much as most of our brothers, sisters, uncles, aunts, mothers, fathers, cousins, nephews, and family members were kidnapped and made slaves in a foreign land – the effects of such an event didn't only affect them, but also affected those who remained behind as much as it affected those who were captured. On top of that, as the Slave trade materialized, different European countries began to come for a complete takeover and annihilation of the Blackman in his land, property, and continent. In South Africa, these slave masters owned prisons, but most importantly, they owned farms. As much as black people who remained were not kidnapped and shipped to different countries through the slave trade; they were instead dispossessed of their property, their religion, their culture, their land, their livestock, their economies, their civilizations and just like our brothers and sisters who were captured as slaves; our mothers, fathers, brothers, and sisters were also raped and murdered against their own will. And those who resisted were either killed, publicly humiliated, burned alive or hanged. This side the situation was even worse, because they killed our leaders, chiefs, kings, and queens and then hanged their heads where everyone could see to spark more fear to further indoctrinate and conquer black people not only physically, but spiritually and psychologically. They were (our ancestors) forced to worship their masters, and in Afrikaans, their "Baas" or Boss. Places, where slavemasters lived here in South Africa, were called farms. But there is no difference between farms and the plantation – two sides of the same coin. But different connotations in different parts of the world identified the latter for their collective comprehension. In South Africa, instead of Africans to be recognized as Negros, the slavemasters identified us as "Kaffirs." Which, just like the Negro, denoted that we were a property of the slave master – but most importantly, we were non-believers (This is according to the slave settlers).

So given the comparative account of the events that took place in the past 300 years, particularly between the United States of America and South Africa, you will then realize that my mother was a slave. The farm she was working for produced coffee beans and tea bags, and according to her explanation – some of her colleagues died while working and was not even allowed to assist those who collapsed for whatever reason.

Growing up in the black community – my experience

I experienced the legacy of White-terror-domination or White supremacy before I could study nor make contact with any White person in the physical. This experience is often relative to most black people because when you grow up black, in supposedly a chiefly and stereotypically brainwashed black community, either in a village or township, there are normally slave stereotypes that you are born into before you can even learn or rather experience the system of White-terror-domination.

Most elders, in most black communities, have inherently promulgated stereotypical and conventional thinking as a result of the multigenerational transmission of slave

VUKULU SIZWE MAPHINDANI | 30

thinking and a depressed psyche resulting from centuries of dehumanization. To most of them, and this is based on my experiences and the experiences of others, everything good has normatively been associated with Whites. When you eat a unique, yet a great dish, they are likely to (most) say that you are eating "White" *(Udya xilungu in Tsonga)*. When you conduct yourself differently and hygienically, they are likely to tell, "You think you are white"; when you are very selective and self-isolating to generally accepted norms, they are likely to say, "You behave like whites and you will never be one of them." So without an anthropological conclusion to this "Kaffir like pathological Slave thinking," it is unhurried to conclude that most blacks (families and communities) in South Africa have been dehumanized into a detached and inferior species with their Humanity and common sense stripped out of their existence. And the idea behind these stereotypes in most cases is that; it's either you fit in and reflect the nature of a kaffir that Verwoerd tried to roast through the bastardized Bantu Educational system or you will suffer the ridicule, in which, if not monitored and managed with caution, it will result in long term grudges with members of one's community. It is mostly black people, who today, after almost four hundred years of menticide and dehumanization teach their children to worship whites from an early age more than whites have recently been doing with their system of psychological remote control because black people are unconsciously defending the idea of inferiority to whites and are as a result treacherous to those who stand up against White psychological, mental, chemical and economic abuse like myself and others.

In my very first published book, Message To The Blackman in Africa, which is a deleterious prospect against mental sickness and a proponent of a newly found Black Consciousness, I shared a letter that was written by Willie Lynch and was delivered as a speech on December 25 in 1712, where Willie Lynch advises the

State of Virginia (In USA) slave owners on how to control and break their black slaves spiritually and psychologically. In February 2020, I traveled to the USA, and I was based in Virginia. However, it was unfortunate that the James River, at the state of Virginia, was closed due to Corona Virus lockdowns as of May 2020 when I left, so I couldn't possibly visit the place. Although Willie Lynch's letter remains subject to further scrutiny, when I read that letter for the first time (in 2012), I was in complete disbelief. What fixed my attention is the emphasis on *"keeping the black slaves mentally weak and physically strong."* The letter remains one of the most significant historical references on the existence of psychological warfare against Black people globally. Today, more than three hundred years later, since the letter was delivered in 1712, the number one resource in the breaking process of the Blackman is the mind; because your brain is your primary weapon of survival, and anyone who psychologically or spiritually messes with it destroys your life. Black people, as subjects of a psychological discourse here in South Africa, continue to be kept as mental slaves and compliant with all the requirements necessary to advance sophisticated and re-inforced systems of psychological programming. Well, the South African slave master also draws his inspiration towards the castigation and the dehumanization of blacks from the systematically bias teachings and convictions of the racist Hendrick Verwoerd. Below is a speech Hendrick Verwoord gave on 7 June 1954 as the then minister of Education (remember, education is instrumental in the orientation or disorientation of one's psyche) this speech was delivered two years after the Bantu Educational system was introduced as a system of education for Blacks only (Kaffirs):

> "It is the policy of my department that education should have its roots entirely in the Native areas and in the Native environment and Native community. There, Bantu education must be able to

give itself complete expression, and there it will have to perform its real service. The Bantu must be guided to serve his own community in all respects. There is no place for him in the European community above the level of certain forms of labour. Within his own community, however, all doors are open.

For that reason, it is of no avail for him to receive a training which has as its aim absorption in the European community while he cannot and will not be absorbed there. Up till now, he has been subjected to a school system that drew him away from his own community and practically (sic) misled him by showing him the green pastures of the European but still did not allow him to graze there. This attitude is not only uneconomic because money is spent on education, which has no specific aim, but it is even dishonest to continue with it. The effect on the Bantu community we find in the much-discussed frustration of educated Natives who can find no employment which is acceptable to them. It is abundantly clear that unplanned education creates many problems, disrupts the communal life of the Bantu, and endangers the communal life of the European. For that reason, it must be replaced by planned Bantu

Education. In the Native territories where the services of educated Bantu are much needed, Bantu education can complete its full circle, by which the child is taken out of the community by the school, developed to his fullest extent in accordance with aptitude and ability and thereafter returned to the community to serve and to enrich it."

Hendrick Verwoerd was clear and evident in his solidification of the complete psychological subjugation of the black "subject" in South Africa, just as his predecessors were. Each generation from the White power structure weighed all forms of evil against us. The result of such an auspicious and a credible system of dehumanization on black people by weaponizing the educational system was and is still significantly beneficial. This creative oppression inspired an increased production in black slave laborers who became nothing but garden boys for white elites, construction workers, housemaids, cleaners, security guards, plumbers, carpenters, farmworkers, sex slaves, bartenders, gamblers, boxers, football players, cashiers, police, etc. and today, that project on psychological remote control and programming has made possible for blacks to perpetuate slave-like psychology which is fueled by the Media subconsciously; News reporting, Television dramas, reality Tv shows and so forth. The television system is weaponized as a programming device against unsuspecting Blacks' subconsciousness. In my upbringing, I recall there was a Television series broadcasted between 1999-2004, Yizo Yizo. The series portrayed and endorsed a negative image of blacks, and it was produced by a well-respected white production company, Bomb productions. The project was written and directed by Angus Gibson, a white male, in partnership with Tebogo Mahlatsi – a Black male. Yizo Yizo depicted blacks as savages, gangs, dysfunctional, and rapists. As a result, the Show producers were later accused by parliamentarians at the time of contributing tremendously to social decay because the first series of that mind-controlling device was spewing subliminal messages and creative means were used to idolize prison and to endorse the public status of gangsters, because prisoners would be coming out of the penitentiary and be controlling the entire community and in the school, henceforth managing teachers, RGB, the principal and raping young female learners, etc.

And even though the producers and directors have put forward a convincing argument claiming that the show was about creating awareness of the black condition at that time, the truth is that the series was creatively used to motivate gangsterism, public dysfunctionality, and self-hatred in the black community. This, I sternly believed that it was responsible for the increased number of black people going to prison between the period 1999-2004 with the desperate guise that they will be feared and well respected when coming out of jail. Just like it was in Yizo Yizo, in most black schools at the time, characters such as "Papa Action" and "Chester" were credibly manifesting in different young black males who solicited the lifestyle precisely as it was portrayed on the series. Black people have given the entire world civilization; we liberated the Whiteman in Europe long before he even knew what civilization was, and we gave the world a more human face, so how is it be possible that today we participate in our demise? How can a people who gave life to Humanity be so dysfunctional today more than they have ever been any time in History? That's because the Whiteman has invested in the control of the Blackman's mind since there won't be any White supremacy without black participation. White Film Producers are investing millions in debunking Black's racial identity. And the media system; through Newspapers, radio shows, Internet (social media) and Television have created a virtual identity or rather the impression that blacks are criminals, and funny enough, Whites control the media system. But how can people who have dehumanized, incarcerated, enslaved, murdered, raped, bombed, stole, etc. portray people who have only accepted Humanity to their home as criminals? Blacks are not inherently criminal; in most cases, they are victims of circumstance (dehumanization or ecocide) who walk around with a systematically engineered psychology, although some commit crimes as a result of starvation and poverty – a direct legacy of colonialism and Apartheid in the absence of reparations.

I've also come to realize that most blacks do not inherently participate in prostitution and drug dealing because they are prostitutes or drug dealers. But most of those who are trapped in this behavior are usually doing so for the benefit of survival in an economic system that was designed to place black people at the bottom of the value chain much that even those who have jobs are poorly paid henceforth making it difficult for them to take care of their loved ones. Let's have a look at a few jobs below and their average salaries:

1. Security Guards typically earns an average salary of R3500,

2. Cleaners = R3500,

3. Construction workers = R2500,

4. Receptionists = R5000,

5. Restaurant waiters/servers = R4000,

6. Call Centre Agents = R3500 + commission

7. Admins/Secretaries = R9000

8. Nurses = R12500.

I can go on and on. This pyramid is randomly evident in black families. And in most cases, if not all, each black employee is likely to have more than four dependents, whether they are married and have children or not. What lately, those who are ignorant enough have come to coin "Black tax." So Almost 50% of prostitutes in South Africa are

Zimbabwean women who, in their search for greener pastures have crossed the border and came to South Africa with the hope of prospering and only to find out that this is a jungle full of self-hatred and starvation and are henceforth left with no other option but to peddle with their bodies for a little dime so that they can be able to send money back home for their children' school fees, groceries and other essentials. The circle is similar to South African prostitutes – the system has placed black people in nearly a permanent state of survival. Most prostitutes come from poor households, and they have babies to feed since many are single parents, although they never make these babies on their own. It is, therefore, challenging for black people to flawlessly become a completely functional racial collective on top of all that we have been through. Three hundred and forty-two years of slave labour, dehumanization, genocide, and mass incarceration, and we are still economic and mental slaves.

Today, more than 360 years later, since

the arrival of Jan Van Riebeek in 1652, we continue to serve the liberal White establishment here in South Africa and wherever black people are concerned. You build them malls, and they call you "Dakaboys," you bath their babies and cook them food, and they call you kitchen girls, you maintain their gardens and fix their pools, and they call you garden boys, you nurture their farms and grow their crops. Still, they sustain the narrative that you are incapable of farming whenever the land debate is concerned - you stand up and demand your dispossessed property, and they call you racist and uncivilized. What have we done to warrant such a perpetual prescription of servitude?

Five hundred years of the black mass incarceration and genocide, and we are still a public enemy. My forefathers, whom we are told have been civilized by European colonialism and invasion although that's not true; were victims of racial oppression, they were invaded; wives raped in front of husbands and the public community, young babies kidnapped and sold as slaves, employees working from sunset until sundown with no pay to develop this colonial cluster with no name, not even a nickname (South Africa). House helpers then were forced to perform blowjobs to their white bosses under the desperate guise that they would lose their jobs should they disobey - and today, the narrative is no different. Black housekeepers continue to do blowjobs to their white bosses; some of them are mandated to have sexual intercourse with their slavemaster's dogs at a salary of R2500 per month, bearing in mind that these exploited employees support large families with some of their children in universities. They are breadwinners in their respective spaces but are drinking from the same well of economic oppression, just like their forefathers and mothers did. So why would you think you think you are free?

On 25 October 2017, times live published the following article:

The Family Violence, Child Protection and
Sexual Offences Detectives in Ekangala
are investigating a case of rape following
the alleged rape of a 41-year-old domestic
worker in Riamar Park, Bronkhorstspruit.
She alleged that on Monday, the 45-year-
old suspect dragged her into a room in the
house, where he allegedly raped her until
the early hours of the next day, police
spokesman Captain Mavela Masondo said
on Wednesday.

This incident happened 23 years after
South Africa's first democratic election. So
what's democratic about black people
castigated to the deepest corners of
economic displacement after suffering for
342 years without reparatory justice?
Back in 2005, another comparable
incident occurred in Johannesburg, where
a maid named Rose (38 years old then)
alleged that her boss had kept her as a sex
slave for three months.

"He forced me to sleep with him. He said
dirty things to me and made me watch
pornography while he raped me. He also
used this on me," she said, pointing to a
red plastic sex aid. Rose also specified

that she was threatened to keep quiet by her boss or else he was going to fire her and ensured that she could not get another job.

"It is further alleged that the suspect then forced the victim to perform sexual acts on his dog. "The police were alerted about this gruesome act and reacted swiftly to arrest the perpetrator," he said.

In a statement, the provincial commissioner of police in Gauteng, Lieutenant General Deliwe de Lange, assured the accuser and her family "that the police will ensure that the suspect is brought to justice, and if found guilty, he must pay dearly for his evil and barbaric acts". On 14 March 2005, the perpetrator was arrested and appeared at the Randburg Magistrate court the following day, but unfortunately, he was granted R5000 bail.

So is this how petty the South African justice system has become, especially as a respected state institution?

Because if the judiciary is compromised, then we might as well kiss our beautiful country goodbye. A bail of R5000? After having held a human being hostage and a sex slave for three f****n months? Maybe we should establish if whether or not the justice system is another money-making machine not interested in justice – but profit-motivated because that's not justice at all. Is it because the woman is black? I don't believe that the odds would have been similar should it have been a white woman kidnapped by a Blackman and continuously raped for three months and dehumanized to have sex with animals. If it were a blackman, he would have probably earned a life sentence if he did that to a White woman. We live in a society where black lives are just as equally recessive as those of animals;

probably animals even receive much better treatment than black people. Rich white people who have acquired their wealth through land dispossession and colonialism can even afford R100 000 bail.

In 2010, SACSIS.org.za released a report that there approximately one million, mainly black women who are domestic workers in South Africa. Reading from a couple of incidents taking place in White families with regards to how they treat their maids, it is concerning to imagine what our mothers are going through in this domestic work industry, and we are living in a free society.

Mineworkers then were forced to work from morning to night with close to no pay as employees of mostly the

DeBeers or Anglo-American and Goldfields mines. They were staying in dusty shacks and plots and were not allowed to visit other places except within their area of work, and the regulatory permit was issued as such. Mineworkers today and recently (2012) were murdered for demanding an increase to their shockingly degenerate salaries, and justice was never served. Every morning I come across black people sitting by the gas station waiting for "Baas" to load them at the back of a truck for any kind of work at any given sum for as long as they will be able to survive. It is, therefore, safe and probable for me to consider myself, and as part of the black racial family an outlaw. I'm a Kaffir, and not because I'm a non-believer or degenerate, but because I inherit the ills of multigenerational transmission of psychological abuse and economic slavery by continuing to serve white masters in a country that was built on the backs of black men and black women.

Whenever I visit Shoprite, pick n pay, McDonald's, Truworths, Woolworths, KFC, and any other White-owned multinationalcorporation/retailer/restaura nt around the country, I continue to see black people working more than ten hours for a minimum wage good enough to last for just about five days. One has to spend the rest of the month waiting for the next pay to enjoy it for just another five days, and then would have to wait again for another month-end, etc. and that probably goes on and on until retirement, and we then leave our babies and generations thereafter without inheritance but poverty and economic exploitation from generation to generation. Freedom is not the right to vote, freedom is not having access to an education that you can't afford and access to areas that you can't even afford to live in with your tiny salary, but freedom is being economically, politically, psychologically, Scientifically free. What will the freedom to vote and move around do to me if I remain an economic, industrial, and psychological slave? This country doesn't even have or instead promotes freedom of speech. I was previously censored by the ENCA in April 2016 in a pre-recorded interview where I shared my views on democracy simply because I had said I don't see myself free for as long as I continue to troll harder for survival. On the 27th of July 2017, I was again censored by the SABC news channel in an interview about my book, Message to the Blackman in Africa with Alicia Jali, the AM live presenter. And although it's somehow discouraging to be pickled like an outcast in your motherland, there is no amount of censorship, hatred, and violent maltreatment that will ever stop me from speaking my mind about the Black condition in this country. Most people even think I'm a hate teacher, but why? Have I ever taught you to hate anyone based on the colour of their skin? Have I ever taught you to kill, incarcerate, dehumanize, indoctrinate, rape, and enslave anyone based on the colour of their skin? So what's hateful about black reeducation? My divine ministry is to teach black people to love themselves after four hundred years of social engineering and miseducation. If asking black people to stop killing, raping and hating themselves is a hate teaching, so let me be that.

Why wouldn't I enlighten my people when job interviews decide our lives? And did you know that we pay more interest than whites from financial institutions like banks on car loans, personal loans, mortgage loans, etc.? Let me tell why. This is because financial institutions/banks employ a credit rating system before any loan can be approved (to assess affordability and capacity to be able to pay back the said loan). The more poor your credit score is, the more interest you are likely to pay. It's unfortunate that black people have the most inferior credit rating of all times because there was nothing to inherit from our parents and their parents and grandparents since they were systematically reduced to economically participate as security guards, gardeners, police, nurses, farmworkers, etc.

Chapter 2

CODESA's negotiations
and the ignored question
of Reparations in South
Africa

t was on the 6th of April in the year 1652, about 368 years ago, when a Dutch descendant in the person of Jan Van Riebeek arrived in Cape Town, South Africa. That very day has had a significant impact on the entire history of South Africa. The arrival of that European and his buddies have, over the years, compromised a once-thriving civilization that elated attractions as Mapungubwe, Adam's calendar, Barberton, amongst others. However, the generally accepted account rigorously privileges the notion that Europe Civilized Africa – an ahistorical illusion. In as much as Europe's falsification of South Africa's history is concerned, the misrepresentation and mis-telling of these elements of our very truth remain secreted amidst the colonizer's quest to justify Colonization, Apartheid, and Slavery in South Africa and to repel the psychological existence of black people further.

By the year 1989, South Africa has headed towards an economic collapse after 338 years of colonial rule. This, of course, was a result of various beasts of burden. Amongst them was the Guerilla Wars waged by liberation groups like the Azanian People's Liberation Army, Poqo and Umkhonto We Sizwe (Amongst others); also, the sanctions raised by the United States Congress and various Superpower countries around the world played a fundamental role. Upon the realization of this sudden catastrophe, the National Party government announced the unbanning of political parties/leaders and the release of political prisoners/exiles. By 1990 the situation had forced the NP government to negotiate with various liberation groups to discuss the country's way forward which was a strategic move to have the sanctions lifted since the sanctions reciprocated preconditions to be honored before they could be lifted – a hegemonic practice that was inherent in the Colonial government/s politics of "self-preservation." So, in short, the defeat of

Apartheid was already inevitable. But economic Hitmen in the form of European Descendants who were already foregrounded on the politics of racialism were not that oblivious to perceive this basic pattern from a far-reaching distance. So in this regard, the Convention for a Democratic South Africa (CODESA) was their very last hope at retaining the upper-class privileges for their future descendants after 389 years (1990) of slogging tooth and nail for the bastardization, dehumanization, enslavement and the extermination of the "Kaffir" in order to copyright South Africa for the benefit of their future generations and not those of the "Kaffir" (Black people in their definition). The very first CODESA meeting took place in the year 1991. Present was the African National

Congress, Inkatha Freedom Party, the National Party, the South African Communist Party, amongst others; this very session was considered the plenary session.

CODESA's negotiations remain a determining factor in today's window dressing democracy. This is because the negotiation inputs were never made public – and thus, the liberation project was compromised although publicly inscribed as the peacemaking settlement. As I was going through a document published on the government website in 2012, I came across a report on Reparations and Rehabilitation from the Government's justice.gov website (I suspect the content was detached). One of the points on the report jagged out that "The Incoming government has accepted the responsibility for reparations." As much as I recognized the fact that the ANC conceded a great deal during CODESA's negotiations, there was no way I would have imagined that they would in their right mind, not only inherit the Apartheid monetary debt across the globe but most importantly – to accept the responsibility for the damage in which they were a victim of. For almost 400 years, European nations, mainly Dutch Descendants and Britain; have enslaved, incarcerated, mass murdered, dehumanized, economically exploited, and raped Africans in this part of the world and in return, instead of repair the unparalleled damage of that gradation, they instead – protected those ills perpetually. And to this day, Black people are still being held economically hostage under the guise of a free market capitalist system, whereas that's nothing but the continued bloodsucking of black people.

It's necessary to assume that we have lost more than a million lives under colonialism and Apartheid crimes and that's genocide. Also, we have lost our wealth, land, property, civilization, and humanity, but despite all that, when the topic of reparatory justice arises – the descendants of white slave masters instead accuse black people of being lazy and dependent to government welfare – such self-immolation. I have never seen such arrogance anywhere else in the world except in cases where black people are involved. When the African National Congress accepted and appropriated the responsibility for reparations and rehabilitation, Colonialism and Apartheid crimes – Desmond Tutu was appointed the Chairperson of the Truth and Reconciliation Commission. The Truth and Reconciliation Commission established The Reparations and Rehabilitation Committee (R&R), and unfortunately, the Committee got suspended in 1998 without producing quantifiable progress. The R&R only accepted individual submissions of those who were directly "attacked" by Apartheid Mafias or those whose loved ones were murdered/raped etc. And most importantly, the Reparations and Rehabilitation Committee only accepted those submissions if the incidents were from 1960 onwards – That was a scam, but instead, the African National Congress approved that. In reality, colonialism in South Africa was not a

1960-1994 event. It was a very prolonged evil era affecting more than eight generations since the arrival of Jan Van Riebeek in 1652, and the process of reparatory justice is not something to be made submissions on, because the United Nations has already laid guidelines in dealing with the question of reparations as a supervisory tool toward affected nations.

Under the guidelines by the United Nations are the following critical steps:

1.   *Restitution:* this refers to measures which "restore the victim to the original situation before the gross violations of international human rights law and serious violations of international humanitarian law occurred," for example, restoration of liberty, enjoyment of human rights, identity, family life, and citizenship, return to one's place of residence, restoration of employment and

return of property (in this regard it's land, wealth and commercial properties).

2. Compensation: "should be provided for any economically assessable damage, as appropriate and proportional to the gravity of the violation and the circumstances of each case, resulting from gross violations of international human rights law and serious violations of international humanitarian law," such as lost opportunities, loss of earnings and moral damage.

3. Rehabilitation: "should include medical and psychological care as well as legal and social services."

4. Satisfaction: is a broad category of measures, ranging from those aiming at a cessation of violations to truth-seeking, the search for the disappeared, the recovery and reburial of remains, public apologies, judicial and administrative sanctions, commemoration and memorialization, and human rights training.

5. Guarantees of non-repetition: is another broad category which includes institutional reforms tending towards civilian control of military and security forces, strengthening judicial independence, the protection of human rights workers, human rights training, the promotion of international human rights standards in public service, law enforcement, the media, industry, and psychological and social services. This, in relation to the Jewish genocide, is the criminalization of anyone who can make public assertions in defense of the Holocaust. So because we never had this in South Africa, we have seen leaders of White South Africa publicly applauding the system of Apartheid, eg. Hellen Zille of the Democratic alliance, Kallie Kriel of Afriforum and FW De Klerk.

These very steps were never considered in the Reparations and Rehabilitation

Committee in South Africa. Adding to this insult was the Committee paying about 17000 families a settlement of R30 000 per family, which, by any means, bear no respect for the process and also, no respect for the entire black humanity. In South Africa today, the land is still in the hands of Whites, the economy in the hands of whites, and the control of goods and the value chain in the hands of Whites.

Here are 8 major banks in South Africa and their ownership:

First National Bank (Private and White-owned)

Standard Bank (Private and White-owned)

Absa (Private and White-owned)

Nedbank (Private and White-owned)

Bidvest (Private and White Owned)

Nedbank (Private and White-owned)

African Bank (Private and White-owned)

Investec (Private and White-owned)

And as the saying goes, those who controls the money controls the Government, so this means, whatever they say goes – and these politicians on our screens are nothing but puppets. The circulation of the South African currency doesn't happen without the knowledge of the aforementioned banks, and none of them is State nor Black-owned. In March 2019, I visited Lilongwe, Malawi. I still remember the events of my first day in the country vividly. As I was hungry and wanted to get something to eat after traveling for about three days by bus with little to eat during my journey, I then asked the owner of the B&B that I rented for the duration of my stay to take me around so that I could get something to eat, possibly a South African equivalent of Pap and beef stew. The owner of the B&B was a 65-year-old retired IT specialist who instead offered to give me a mini-tour, although it was about 9 pm. As he was taking me to the nearest hotel to get something to eat, we passed via an ATM so that I could withdraw some Malawian Kwacha just in case I could experience issues with my South African VISA bank card at the hotel.

The nearest ATM, about 7 minutes drive from the B&B, was by a bank named NBS Bank limited. At first, I never really paid attention to the bank ownership because we in South Africa have many banks, with none of them owned by Black people. But out of curiosity, I so happened to ask about the ownership of the bank, and the gentleman, my host, advised that it was owned by a Blackman named Vizenge Kumwenda. I was shocked for a moment, considering the fact that Malawi is a landlocked country with limited economic activities but a Blackman in that country was owning a bank, which is doing good by the way – this was interesting because it meant that, even though they are having economic difficulties, they still had a say in the circulation of their currency. Well as if that was not enough, the following day I withdrew money from a bank named Eco bank, which I was told, although not owned by a Malawian National, it was definitely owned by a Blackman named Emanuel Ikazoboh. It is a Pan-African bank for that matter – okay, this to me was fascinating. On my third day, again, I withdrew money in area 6, Lilongwe from a bank named FDH bank Limited, this time around, I was moving round Lilongwe with a driver who hardly understood English and I never really bordered to ask a thing to avoid the perpetuation of an already existing language barrier. So, unfortunately, my bank card was swallowed by the ATM. At this point I'm frustrated because I hadn't bought my bus ticket home, and I still had about seven more days to stay, and that was my only South African bank account. So we informed the security of the challenge at hand, and they requested for my passport, I gave it to them – and 10 minutes later they came back with my card, this was amazing. And again, I was prompted to ask about the ownership of the bank, and I was told that it belonged to a Blackman by named Mark Mikwamba. I was never this impressed by Black nationalist thinking of this magnitude ever. And the following morning, I came to learn that almost 70% of Malawian Petrol stations were owned and controlled by black people, and so, I was profoundly troubled.

Because, I then reflected broader when coming home, that in my country, all banks are White-owned. All petrol stations (White-owned). All major food stores (White-owned). Major Clothing factories (White-owned). Major insurance businesses (White-owned). All Cellphone networks (White-owned). Commercial properties (90% white-owned) and I had to think again and again about CODESA's negotiations where everything happened. Yes, the acquisition of White economic power in South Africa happened during the 342 years of White rule. Still, most importantly, the sustainability of this phenomenon was endorsed by the African National Congress during CODESA's negotiations, and out of all African countries, we are the only country that's not truly liberated. Yes, of course, the infrastructure is good, just like in all countries built out of slave labour, but our infrastructure is not so different from the fake life people portray on social media while dealing with the worst in their day to day lives. We lease our properties from them (Preceding colonialists). If lucky enough to buy the land, we will build our houses using blocks of cement purchased from them and all the equipment, so we cannot be liberated until we realize and accept that we are still slaves in the land of our forefathers, who thrived in every aspect of life until European Colonization, miseducation, and Television. Since then, they were bastardized to reflect backwardness.

What's the solution?

Any political party that goes into Government, primarily if interested in social justice, needs to solicit the ignored question of reparations when drafting a way forward for South Africa. In a couple of instances, I have argued that reparatory justice is one fundamental and rather a critical solution to South Africa's question of inequality – which is a byproduct of Colonialism and Apartheid. This will help ease the slowly burning desire for civil war. Having one race on top of the other is mental sickness, and retaining such a bubbling status quo will lead us to an anarchic genocide.

A reparatory educational system

Black Consciousness, therefore, is necessary for the psychological re-orientation of black minds from early childhood development. For example, the most critical tool that was completely destroyed throughout the 342 years was the mind. So the educational system must be converted into a rehabilitation and skills centre for both black and white children. As much as white children have been psychologically miseducated to believe that they are superior to blacks, Black children were systematically miseducated to believe in the inferiority complex, much that 400 years later – we are dealing with a compromised social order working towards the maintenance of White terror domination and Black ecocide (Economic genocide).

For example, since South Africa thrives in Gold, Manganese, diamond, platinum, and chromium mining, the educational system must be designed to maximize on our Gross Domestic Product (Skills set). But most importantly, a child from Grade 1 till Grade 5 must only study African history, Economics, Mathematics, Land literature and their choice of specialty. Then from Grade 6 to 12, they will take on from their specialty. Specialties may include, Mining, Production, Business

Management, Information and Technology, Astrology, Geography, Land literature, Science, and so forth. All the above are within the confines of the South African state; it's economy, it's resources, land and practical enough to help maximize the economic growth than study "Photosynthesis" your whole primary and secondary education and still have to go to university and be treated as an empty vessel. What is the purpose of the 12 years of schooling if one will even need to go to university? Primary and secondary education is enough to serve as a University exemption if the educational system correctly equipped.

Economy

As much as the Apartheid economy thrived in the confiscation of black people's property for White people's benefit and Black slave labour, in about 400 years, it has placed White people at the top of the economic chain because they have a sovereign government and henceforth, sovereign economic system. This time around, we need to recover the sovereignty of our economic system. For example, all banks that were established with the help of the colonial Government are inherently a State institution. All mining, all superpower corporations that were established with the support of the Colonial government, need to be reclaimed. Land rights must belong to the Government and no one else, henceforth, those who use the land for commercial purposes will need to pay Land tax, and also, if the commercial land is used for mining, then the state will have shares on same.

In Conclusion, once the question of education is solved, and the economic problem resolved too; everything else will fall into place because we have gotten used to suffering in the hands of White Domination for 400 years now, which was also preceded by the Arab enslavement of mostly Northern parts of Africa. **ALL POWER TO THE PEOPLE!!!**

Chapter 3

Our trailing State of Blackness

I t is anticipated that the result of the current state of Unconsciousness in the Black community will be significantly manifested in their sense, or loss of sense, of heritage; their feeling, or lack of feeling, of being a people with a robust and unique sense of their own Humanity. With this lost sense of heritage, the Blackman finds himself in a world very strange toward him, a world that is continuously furnished and decorated in which he cannot make his unique contribution because he has lost a sense of his Blackness. The picture continues to be painted without Blackness; hence the world is forever strange to Black people. He has to be taught how to live in it, how to express his Blackness in it, how to behave in it, how to speak in it. This eventually leads to the dissolution of his heritage, his sense of Humanity, and the emergence of a pre-defined heritage and humanity by those who are actively involved in the furnishing of this world since the slave trade and colonialism. A writer once said, "...in an effort to destroy completely the structures that have been pre-built in global Black Communities and to impose their imperialism with an unnerving totality, the colonialists were not satisfied merely with holding a people in their grip and emptying the Native's brain of all forms and content, they turned to the history (and related sources) of the oppressed and distorted, disfigured and destroyed it. No longer was there a reference made to Black people's culture;

it converted to barbarism. Africa became the 'dark continent.' Religious practices and customs were denoted as superstition. The history of Black People got reduced to tribal battles and internal wars...No wonder a Black child learns to hate his heritage in his days at school. So contrary is the image presented to him that he tends to find solace only in close identification with White people."

The Whiteman has managed to convince the Blackman that the way he (the white man) lives is the right way to live, the things he does are the right things to do, the way he is and behaves is the right way to be and behave and that virtually everything about him is correct, and that the Blackman must learn his ways; learn to live in his world, because his world "is" the way things are, and the Blackman is still unlearned. So the Blackman then enters the playing field pre-determined by the Whiteman, who has created and has been playing the game for a long time and is more experienced. This is a complex game where the rules and skills of survival must be learned over time - since the Blackman is new, it is expected of him to lose. Because White People and other nations have created the game and set the rules of this very game – while Black people were enslaved after our Civilization was invaded over 2000 years ago, so these groups are more experienced in the contemporary game, they play it far better than the Blackman; they are more equipped to be actively involved in the development and evolution of the game. The problem is that, in this situation, white people begin to attribute their superiority in this very game to their skin colour (Which is a questionable aspersion since their wealth or conceived supremacy is an ill-gotten result, in this instance, the Blackman was cheated). They start to convince themselves that they are better at this game because they are white and superior. Similarly, Black people begin to attribute their inferiority (a direct result of slavery and colonization) in the game to their skin colour. They start accepting and henceforth believing that they are inferior because they are Black. This situation creates a superiority-inferiority complex between Blacks and Whites. With this kind of belief, the Blackman finds himself an eternal student to the Whiteman as Steve Biko elaborated. He finds himself always a few (or many) steps behind the Whiteman, and he starts to measure his sense of Humanity against how well he plays the game as compared to the Whiteman. When he sees, of course, that the Whiteman still plays it better, he flinches that there's something wrong about him, something defective; "why can't I play the game as the Whiteman does?" What's wrong with me? Because white people have been more involved in the development and evolution of this game over the years while Black people were robbed of the opportunity to do so, it is logical that the features of the game will be in favour of white people. Many things in the game will be white more than they are Black in a continent native to Black people. So the Blackman virtually finds himself playing the Whiteman's game – where he hasn't made his African input to swerve the odds in his favour. This game is called modern civilization according to White people's disconcerted and misguided worldview.

In this game, all things that relate to the Whiteman and his community have been labeled "civil," and all things that relate to the Blackman and his community have been labeled "barbaric" – one of the rules mastered by white people. So the only way the Blackman can live and thrive in this world is if he begins to live like the White man and abide by the rules he has set. Science, commercialized sport, technology, medicine and all seem to have been created by the Whiteman (which is the idea that white people have successfully managed to portray by erasing the achievements of Black people and distorting our history), so it doesn't take much to convince the Blackman that he is 'defective.' This feeling of 'defectiveness'; of longing to be like the white man signals itself in the way Black people speak, dress, act, think, behave, and Live. The problem is not that White people have termed Black people's culture barbaric; the problem is that Black people believe White people, to the extent that they start seeing things the way they do, they also begin to see themselves as primordially barbaric, primitive, inferior and as having to progress to become more 'civil.' They use white people's lens through which they perceive and measure themselves.

I perceive modernity as a homogenous system comprised only of the

Whiteman's tradition, cultures, and ideas that were imposed upon other nationalities under the mask of "development, democracy, and progress." To briefly substantiate the notion that civilization is White culture: English is regarded by many as "the language of man." If you learn English, you have learned along with it the basic ways to live/survive in this world. The same language this book had to be written in if it must reach many readers. And a language characterizes a people. The English language, the language of modernity, is basically representative of White People. And if it is the "language of man" then "man" must surely be White!

Have you ever questioned why on

TV programmes, in books, magazines, the only people that are said to have a "rich culture" are always non-white? Or realized that it is always white tourists who marvel at the cultural richness of other nations? Everywhere you go, every place you visit, every traveling experience story you watch or listen to being broadcasted on TV and radio; the odds are - it is always white people complimenting in awe the cultural richness of non-white people – you will rarely hear a black tourist saying, "Wow, the place was great; the white people there are so rich in culture." It is nearly always a story of, "Wow, the place was great; the infrastructure; the city life and the transport system is so convenient." You will seldom see the Blackman admiring in awe the cultural richness of a white person. If you go to Brazil, China, India, the Middle East, and many other non-white countries, you will realize the direct relationship that exists between "countries predominantly populated by non-whites (non-white countries)" and their spontaneous cultural heritage which distinguishes them from the world.

This presents an apparent dichotomy: The white man always appreciates the cultural richness of non-white groups; the Blackman always appreciates the advancements in civilization (infrastructure, transport systems, etc.) of white groups. However, the Whiteman perceives non-white cultures as outstanding and distinguished not because he is culturally dead, but because his culture is the background, the basis, in which these cultures exist according to his own distorted worldview of Supremacy. Other cultures are outstanding because he is the norm in which the outstanding-ness takes place. His culture, way of life, is the ground from which other cultures protrude. If one carefully analyses modernity, one realizes that it's comprised of nothing or little that is African or Indian or Brazilian or Chinese, etc. in terms of narrative, although the Civilization of Humanity is a result of Black people's arts and sciences, in essence. Almost all nations in the world are concerned with being conservative and preserving their cultures, hence identities, including the Boers/Afrikaners, except many white nations. If modernity was inclusive of all cultures and a blend thereof, as should be a culture that is a governing basis of all modern-life, then such paranoia about conservativeness wouldn't exist amongst so many people. If we all felt that this global culture was equally representing us, then we would all be content to embrace this culture as our own, rather than to develop defense mechanisms against the supposed Western modernity.

This suggests that modernity isn't a realization and a blend of the world's various cultures; it favours Western parts of our global community more than others. The only part that seems not to be concerned about the preservation of its culture or being conservative. In this "civilization," the white man will always have an advantage insofar as Blacks, and other nationalities don't adjust it to give it a more African face. As long as Black people perceive eating with a fork and knife as a new normal, and eating with bare hands as being uncivilized; or purchasing medicines at a clinic as being normal and using natural herbs, as Blacks have always done long before the Whiteman, as abnormal – basically, as long as they continue to perceive and value everything from the perspective of modernity – the white man will always have an advantage. They will end up perceiving their very own selves from that viewpoint – if they haven't done so already – and learn to hate their heritage, because from the white man's view, the position that is modernity, blackness is a stamp through which shame thrives. This is where the system encouraged by civilization meets mental slavery, which I describe as Unconsciousness - that a lost sense of identity exists. Chinese, Indians,

Pakistanis, Brazilians, seem to be gradually developing a unique sense of their own Humanity and are proudly radiating with a strong sense of their own Human personality, but Africans, owing to the state of their collective consciousness or rather, unconsciousness, seem to wear the badge of their culture and heritage with a slender degree of embarrassment and shame. It seems that they believed White people when they said: "Black people's culture is barbaric; Modernity is the way 'real people' live." And this falsehood, and their belief thereof, has had vast effects in the Black community; they have given up their rich African Heritage, sacrificed it, for the adoption of Modernity − European culture. This has led to their suffering. They lead their Black lives using

Modernity as the primary frame of reference from which they perceive and judge themselves and their lives, and if one of them doesn't meet the standards of that measuring rod, they are deemed 'uncivil.' This would have been fine if being Black was epitomized in the global culture, but it isn't.

They have confused their enslavement with their Humanity. By this, I mean that they have grown such reliable identification with their late-history of subjugation that it became a source from which they gain a sense of themselves. The paradox is that they end up hating themselves because they are not their true selves, owing to a false source. They become their own worst enemy in the quest for true Humanity, and they desperately seek an identity, any identity, to which to cling – even if it means ascertaining whiteness their destiny – self-destruction. No wonder they want to live like them, act like them, think like them, speak like them, befriend them, look like them, even have hair that looks like them – even if it means that they lose their own sense of Heritage and true identity in the process.

The fractionalization of the Black Community

During Apartheid, Black communities shared the culture of Ubuntu, brotherhood, and sisterhood; a community was a family as it should be today. A mother of her children was also a mother of her neighbor's children. Community members were familiar with one other.

They greeted each other on the streets or over the fences/walls in the spirit of recognizing their common Humanity, and in some Black communities, people didn't even have to lock their houses - because a Blackman stealing from another was the same as a brother stealing from his own family. They shared everything they had with each other – one wouldn't go hungry while another had food. This was our culture – our Ubuntu – and a significant part, though not absolute, of our heritage. This oneness served as the backbone of the moral fibre in the Black Community, our distinguishing mark as a people - our identity. However, the white man's culture was totally different from ours. In the white community, it was, and still is, highly probable that the neighbors don't know each other on a personal level or even know each other's names; they didn't/don't delightfully greet each other on their streets, over their fences/walls as Black people do. They don't share mutual trust within their communities as much as Black people do; they are a very apprehensive people, unlike Black people, who were/are very trusting, open, and welcoming people. White people don't know what Ubuntu is; it's still probably safe to say that they yet don't know and still learning.

However, the post-Apartheid era has produced a Black community different from the one that once was. The post-apartheid period has seen the fractionalization of Black communities. Before their "freedom" in 1994, Black South Africans had common ground on which to interact and empathize with one another – the common struggle that faced them all. However, they also shared a common "inherent dysfunction": inferiority complex; a hatred for the conditions they were forced to live in, a restlessness within themselves to break away from slavery, an "uncomfortability" with their state of Blackness. When they received their liberation in 1994, the inevitable happened: There are those Blacks who were able to emancipate themselves from this "restlessness," owing to their access to economic and other opportunities, hence breaking identification with it easier. Then there were those Africans that couldn't acquire access to the same resources, hence emancipation, and we are still 'stuck' in the "restlessness"; hence it was more difficult for them to break identification with it. Those that were emancipated broke their identification with slavery and the conditions thereof; those that weren't still identified with slavery and the conditions thereof – of course, except for a few exceptions. There was a minority of rare individuals whose sense of self wasn't drawn from the conditions around them, but from a deeper source within them; the power that lies within each of us that is who we all are. This ultimately led to the fractionalization of the Black community.

The "emancipated black" broke identification with slavery and the conditions thereof; however, most of them identified the Black community in isolation with that "restlessness" and suffering which they rejected – seemingly forgetting that they are also Black and form part of that very community. And so whatever they choose to identify the community from which they come from, they are also, to some degree, invariably choosing to identify with that very same thing themselves. They moved from one form of mental slavery (identification with slavery and the conditions thereof) to another form of mental slavery. The "non-emancipated blacks" remained subject to identification with slavery and the conditions thereof; hence when they looked at the "emancipated," they felt a deep admiration for them and wished to be more like them. This was the beginning of fractionalization: If one section of a society reveres another (and the reverence is not mutual) and 'wants to be like' the other then that means there's a difference between the section that admires and the one that's admired — it means that a homogeneous Society now turns into a heterogeneous Society, comprised of two different parts. This would be healthy if the "emancipated" helped to emancipate their "non-emancipated" counterparts; if they stuck to African tradition and showed pride in their Blackness. The "emancipated," in this role, they would be leading the Black Community, collectively. However, this is not the case because instead of guiding the "non-emancipated" toward their true liberation as well, the "emancipated" judge and condemn them. Instead of using their newly acquired economic resources and accessibility thereto develop, improve, and invest in the Black community, they instead use it to fit into the White community. When the "non-emancipated" recognize this, they begin to feel that they're being treated indifferently by their "emancipated" counterparts; they feel that they have been classed as a different kind of Black people separate from the "emancipated." As a consequence, they begin to act, speak, and think like victims of an 'unfair' economy and society – and this perpetuates poverty, unemployment, and many other socio-economic issues. "They have forgotten where they come from; they're acting white now; they have forgotten us", seems to be their attitude. Many Black people will agree to that saying as I'm sure many of us have heard this in villages and the townships.

The "emancipated" see the "non-emancipated" as 'deliberate' expressions of mental slavery, but instead of making them aware of this, so as to overcome it, they condemn them; the "non-emancipated" see the "emancipated" as moving away from the essence of Blackness and heritage and substituting that with white traditions but instead of helping them become aware of it, by proudly modeling that African way of Life themselves, to set an example, they condemn the "emancipated" and act like victims to their lost sense of Blackness. Both groups derive a false sense of self from seeing themselves as "better" than the other group, or by making themselves "right" and the other group "wrong." A scenario illustrating this in our time would be, for example, Blacks living in the townships or rural areas condemning Blacks living in the suburbs as being "white people in Black skins" or "Oreos" (as they call it), and Blacks living in the suburbs condemning Blacks living in the townships/rural areas as "ignorant and lazy." The irony is that both groups are right, to some degree: Many Blacks living in the suburbs have become like the coconut; equally, many Blacks living in the townships/rural areas have become victims of their own selves and their own minds. The commonly diagnosed problem of the capitalist way of life is that it stresses on the individual and not the collective, which is totally foreign to our Black traditions and way of life. Therefore, Blacks living in the suburbs don't feel any obligation to assist in the emancipating of the "ignorant and lazy" Africans in the townships/rural areas and vice-versa. Capitalism, and also the white tradition, creates a "they" and not a "we" attitude – this is a state of unconsciousness. And the more Blacks live in this kind of system without strong cultural proximity, the more they will lose a sense of their cultural heritage as a people – their Humanity. The African way of Life is based on an "us"; not a "you" or "they".

'Black' jokes

Another manifestation of the deep loss of the sense of Blackness in the Black Community expresses itself in the modern teenager's casual conversations and so-called "Black jokes" he/she makes around his/her circle of friends – whether they be African or white. This also applies to adults, but I have experienced it more from teenagers and young adults or from my own circle of friends – even from myself sometimes. There seems to have developed, over a certain time period, conventional 'jokes' revolving around the Blackman and/or his Society. These 'jokes' are more condescending than funny; more insulting to Black people than humorous. The worst thing is that these very same jokes are articulated by Black people themselves, and it has become normal and socially acceptable to articulate them. To give you an idea of what I'm talking about, here are some of the jokes made that ridicule the Black community (they are explained further down):

1.   "Yoh! Dankie ya munhu wantima!"

2.   "Yes, of course he can't swim; he's African."

Other remarks that usually follow after something negative or bad has happened are:

3. "Eish...muntima yena!"

4. "Eish...Mara African people!"

5. "I swilo swa valungu!"

6. "It's White people's things.'

I once also stumbled upon a t-shirt written: "African people Lafosta." (Meaning: African people, you're forcing it.)

The first point is basically trying to convey a message about the supposed "ungratefulness of the Blackman." It is usually uttered by Black people when they have done something (a favour, an act of kindness, etc.) for another fellow Black and he/she supposedly doesn't react in a way that shows gratitude and appreciation or doesn't reflect what we perceive as acts of gratitude and appreciation. For example: When I was still in high school, one of my classmates lent her textbook to another, and the other promised that she would return it before the end of the school day to my classmate. Only the next day, in class, did the other return it; apologizing for the inconvenience; she said she forgot all about it. My classmate abruptly and sarcastically replied, "I understand, ke dankie ya Mosotho." (Meaning: I understand; that's how African people say thank you). And everybody burst out in laughter, including my two classmates, at this supposed "joke" – all of them Black. As you can imagine I was shocked. What does this all mean?

The second point articulates a truth: Yes, generally, Black people can't swim – they can't deny that, and from my experiences talking with many of them, they don't deny it. The problem is not that Black people generally can't swim; it is the attitude and Consciousness from which that comment emanates. I mean, not knowing how to swim is only as much a problem in the black community as not knowing how to dance and move rhythmically is a problem in the White community. And equally, White people can't deny that – they lack rhythm and really can't dance. It's just not in them; the same way that swimming is just not in us. The problem is the way Blacks speak of themselves as not knowing how to swim: They speak of it as if it's a 'disadvantage' or as if it makes them a lesser capable people than White people. Then, they cover this up with the mask of "joking about it." They do this owing to the dysfunction I spoke of earlier – of using White standards as the standards against which they measure and judge themselves. These "jokes" reflect a lack of pride and sense of Humanity among a people. Ironically, a people so rich in culture and heritage should be the ones at the forefront, modeling national pride and inspiring other nationalities to do the same – not the other way around. The White community does not self-condemn because it can't dance; we should not condemn ourselves that we can't swim. And it's not that we can't; it's that generally, Black people are not interested in learning how to swim or in teaching their children how to swim – whereas white people do. So it is not a matter of being unable; it is simply a matter of interest. The third and fourth points can be explained by referring to the explanation about the first point. They're basically the same. The fifth point, "I swilo swa valungu" ("It's white people's things") reflects the misperception that African people are less knowledgeable and less capable than White people; it also exposes the lie that Black people have made little or no contributions to the development of the world we live in. If a young Blackman sees that a white man, for example, doesn't know how to operate a piece of technology, let's say a remote controller, he will humbly assist, without commentary, and teach the white man how it works. However, if the same thing happens, but this time instead of a white man, it's the Blackman who doesn't know how to operate the device, another Blackman will assist and thereafter feel the need to comment and attribute "not knowing how the remote controller works" to Blackness. When a white person doesn't know, it is "Okay; I mean, he doesn't work here, or he just bought it"; but when an African doesn't know, it is attributed to his Blackness; "He doesn't know because he's Black; these are white people's things!"

The state of Blackness has been so bastardized in the past that Black people now find comfort in associating everything negative and bad with it. So they unconsciously associate themselves with those things. It is 'normal' to do so, and they are comfortable doing it, either because they, themselves, believe, in some twisted logic, that they are separate from that Blackness which they associate with negativity. They have somehow convinced themselves that, "Yes, the state of Blackness is negative, bad, but we are none of those things." This reflects a confused state — a confusion which is a result of a people with no sense of their own Humanity – not because they don't have it; but because they have never defined it. Either that or many Black people still identify with slavery and the conditions thereof. The 'Black people Lafosta' t-shirt, in this context, is the most blatant expression of mental slavery through the mask of "joking about it." To a white reader "Black people, you're forcing it" may have no significance; he may not comprehend what that could be referring to; however, to the African reader, it makes perfect sense because his own community has conditioned his mind in such a way that beholding and receiving insults about his People is as "okay", sane and funny. For the sake of clarity; Black people, you're forcing it or Black people, Lafosta basically means the following: It is an allusion in the Black community that chiefly tries to bear the message that Blacks are not good enough – that greatness and excellence is not their thing. In pursuing it they are trying to ascertain Whiteness. In other words, it is saying that being great is a White thing and attributes everything that is not outstanding and/or not dazzling to being Black. If the Blackman is 'great and brilliant' either in his abilities, talents, or lifestyle, then he is perceived as pretending to be White and out of tune with his Blackness. This is basically what the t-shirt is saying. I feel here that I need not explain further. You, the reader, can, by Now, independently identify the course thereof and the unconsciousness that's heavily-laden on the t-shirt—worst of all, worn by a young Blackman.

Socio-economic issues and Africans

The fractionalization of the black community; hence the collapse of Africans' moral fibre, along with the Ghetto culture and the general cultural feeling in Black communities, has produced an environment conducive to the ascendance of many socio-economic issues faced in South Africa: teenage pregnancy, drug use, alcohol abuse, lack of education, crime, rape, unemployment, etc. These matters are not a cause in themselves but are a result of Consciousness and the cultural sensation/environment produced by that Consciousness in a community. Matters such as crime, teenage pregnancy, drug use, alcohol abuse, and rape – in other words, matters that are solely precipitated and caused by the individual with the intent of harming another or oneself, independent of any external factors – are clearly a reflection of the Consciousness or 'soul-condition' of that individual; such matters are self-induced. Unemployment, lack of education and other related issues – unlike the other issues mentioned above – are external, macro-environmental factors and can't be said to have been caused solely by the individual; the economy plays a role since it is an inherited and socially isolated Apartheid economy. So many of our socio-economic issues are a result of the Consciousness of the communities in which those issues exist; government and NGO's have never understood that. They have always been busy dealing with the results of the true cause and then wonder why they never seem to solve the problems they intend to solve. Feeding schemes are necessary, but they're only effective if tied with workshops, talks, and projects aimed at capacitating, empowering, and fueling Black communities with their own pride, a unique sense of their humanity – by making them feel that they are worth something. Many communities in which socio-economic issues are eminent are usually those where the members of the community have no sense of self-worth; they feel that they have nothing to lose, so "why not have sex at age 13, or abuse drugs?" – they have lost a sense of hope, for themselves and their country. This hopelessness, this lack of a sense of humanity, is what produces the slave-conditions in many of our communities. And when a society begins to identify with these conditions; begins to associate who they are with these conditions because they have been so familiar to them, you get the perpetuation of these conditions in that community; you get mental slavery of Unconsciousness. As long as this psychological bankruptcy continues to exist within that community, then those conditions will also continue to exist. The problem then is not the conditions but the way people think, and the way to solve the problem is not by attacking the conditions but by changing the way people think. Such is the state of many Black communities, and such is the way it needs to be addressed – through Spiritual Consciousness. The South African Government needs to start acknowledging and accepting that so that we may alleviate many of the problems that exist in black communities.

Chapter 4

Ghetto Culture; The School and The Community

here has developed among Black youth in South Africa a trend, a lifestyle, a culture termed 'Ghetto' – to overstand, one has to interpret this connotatively. This culture is rife in many Black communities and many schools thereof; it appears that many young Black South Africans have associated this culture with being Black; hence they identify with this culture. To give a brief description of this culture regarding its identity: Followers of this culture normally wear three-quarter grey trousers (school trousers), white socks and peculiar caps/hats to school or usually extremely tight, short skirts with heavy make-up and hair dyes, if they're female and they graduate from school, the attire follows the same pattern. Of course, this doesn't look presentable. However, that's not the actual problem; the actual problem is that these learners know that they don't look presentable, nor neat and tidy, that they, themselves, can't proudly and openly live out this culture without feeling self-conscious, guilty and ashamed of themselves. However, they continue to try and embrace it because they don't know a life outside the confinements of this culture. This culture has become their identity, and whether it is good or bad, it gets them going.

We all require an identity, and when the community in which you live has lost a sense of its own, you are bound to go look elsewhere for something – anything – you can identify with, so that you may gain a sense of "self." This is what Francois-Marie Arouet (also known as Voltaire) also referred to by saying, "If God didn't exist, man would have to invent Him." He principally tries to show that Man has a strong need to have a sense of belonging – whether it is a belonging to a deity, a family or a culture – and where there is nothing to belong to, Man will create something to which he can belong. So followers of the ghetto culture cannot be blamed much. These are young, lost souls in Black communities that are looking for something – anything – which will give them a sense of belonging – a choice between what's right and what's wrong is a luxury they can't afford; they have to make whatever they find useful. And in this regard - they have discovered the ghetto culture.

I've lived in both rural and township communities and have spent time talking to people who follow this culture; most of them smoke, are performing poorly at school, are sexually active, abuse alcohol and are involved in township street politics – by street politics, I mean gangs and the activities thereof, excessive partying, etc. this is their way of life, and they don't know any other. It is clear, then, that this 'Ghetto' culture isn't conducive to excellence – whether it be academically or in other areas outside of academics; that it isn't helpful to a bright economic future, on the contrary, it inculcates a criminal psyche. And still, it is what young Black youth identify with – slavery and the conditions thereof, just in a new face. This culture is then perpetuated utilizing a role-modeling system: Young, Black children, see their brothers and/or sisters embracing this culture as a way of life and end up believing it is the way life is supposed to be; hence they also grow up to embrace the same culture – unless they're privileged enough to be exposed to a different way of life – and so the cycle continues. This makes Black communities a breeding ground for some, if not many, of the socio-economic issues faced in South Africa. It is a result of Unconsciousness before it is of economic dislocation.

Lived out this way, the Ghetto culture then becomes a blunt manifestation of the mental slavery that's still perpetuated in the Black community. On the one hand, this culture signifies the confused state that black youth are in, owing to the state of unconsciousness of the society from which they come; it signifies a cry for help. On the other hand, it's a reflection of that very state of unconsciousness that Black youth are in: It's evident that though it gives them an identity; it doesn't provide them with a sense of their own Humanity. When they see white children or other Black children that live in the townships but attend school in the suburbs and who do not follow this culture, they deeply admire them; they wish to be like them, and when the realization that they can't arrive humbles them, you can see, in their faces, a deep-felt sorrow – "Why can't I be like that?" They are trapped in their Unconsciousness. I once asked one of them how they would react if they were to see a white teenager dressed the same way as they do, and they burst out in laughter, "That's impossible! Imagine; a white boy in this kind of clothing?" The overall response conveys the message that white people are 'too good for this'; they would never do it, but it's okay for Black people to do it, it's understandable, acceptable and expected of a black teenager to dress inappropriately to school, to be sexually active, to smoke, to abuse alcohol etc. "because that is what they're worth."

This further promotes the idea that greatness is a white thing, and slavery and the conditions thereof is a Black thing. These young black fellows feel that it's okay for them to follow the Ghetto culture because they are not exceptional and bright – unlike white people. They are admitting and accepting, unconsciously, that they are a lesser people. The very minute that a young black decides to follow this culture, he/she has admitted to and accepted that he/she is somewhat inferior to a white person — whether consciously or unconsciously. However, it is necessary here to separate issues: Ghetto-ness, in itself, is not negative or neither is it a slave-culture; it is the way the Black community lives it out that portrays negativity and slave-like. If being ghetto was met by a conscious mind, we would probably get out of it a beautiful and modern version of an ancient African heritage and Civilization. Young, Black South Africans will become the leaders of signifying Blackness in our modern society and how we can live it out. All they need is correct channeling. Culture is a matter of Consciousness. The task that lies before the black community is how they can model the Ghetto culture in a way that encourages Greatness and distinctiveness?

Lost Black Youth

I am afraid that many years from now if a concerted effort isn't exerted towards Consciousness, South Africa, and eventually, the rest of the continent will have a complete Western face, if not a white face. Globalization and neoliberalism have produced a new global culture, where we no longer see Black or White but just an individual. In a positive light, this culture breaks limitations and boundaries that keep Man separated and indifferent toward himself; however, the loss of this Blackness or White-ness has also meant the substitution of Black or White values with Western values – the exalting and glorification of money. This worshiping of money is typically tied up with women, sex, and discourteous language. The culture is modeled by Western Hip Hop celebrities, who are mostly Black and globalized by mass media – which the average teenager is very susceptible and exposed to.

These Black celebrities have already lost a sense of their Blackness, their African-ness and have led their 'disciples,' which are mostly Black teenagers to the same loss. No wonder it has become a norm amongst Black youth in South

Africa to swear, to be sexually active, to dress in a way that is too revealing; no wonder this is regarded as being 'cool.' South Black African youth has been led to crucifying African values – where the emphasis is placed on modesty, humility, our common humanity, Ubuntu – to adopting Western values – where the emphasis is placed on money, sex and objectifying women – and Black parents and leaders have observed and called this normal.

Black youth fall more prone to this for the same reason that black youth in black communities fall prone to the Ghetto culture. The Society to which they belong has lost a sense of its Heritage; its humanity, its unique sense of identity – and where there is no identity, one will desperately go look elsewhere for something, anything, that he can identify with, in order so that he may gain a sense of "self"; a sense of his own humanity — whether it be good or bad. Like those who follow the Ghetto culture, they can't be blamed much. These are young, lost, black souls that are looking for something — anything — which will give them a sense of belonging — a choice between what's right and what's wrong is a luxury they can't afford; they have to make whatever they find right. And they have discovered Western culture — fully endorsed by Black Western celebrities whom they perceive as role models, whether consciously or unconsciously. Black Western celebrities such as Jay-Z, Lil Wayne, Chris Brown, etc. have completely lost a sense of their

Blackness; they have been used by white corporates as a staging point for the bastardization of the Black culture and the glorification of Western culture. They, and the rest of the African world of course, haven't realized it because they're so consumed by the aura of 'wealth' and fame that surrounds them while the white corporates make the real money. It is a concert organized by white people, but where performers and the audience is Black, and while the performers and audience are stuck in that concert drama, the Black community and its culture are being bastardized, crucified, and the Whiteman is getting richer. These Black Western celebrities are lost sunflowers, without a face – neither white nor Black. And they are as lost, if not more lost, as the Black youth they have led to the same facelessness – without a heritage; without a humanity.

However, this need not be the case. Hip hop celebrities are influential in sending out specific messages to their followers – mostly the youth. And if only they could be conscientised and start spreading Black Consciousness, that would revolutionize the Black community.

Chapter 5

Black is beautiful

The word Black is generally perceived as unfavorable by Society in general because of the many negative connotations it has been associated with. Blackness, both literally and figuratively, is conventionally associated with dirt, evil, darkness, slavery, and the conditions thereof. These many negative labels have induced people, especially Blacks, that black is not beautiful – to the extent that they want to separate themselves from the state of Blackness. It is as if you are insulting someone nowadays when calling them Black; it is as if you are looking down on them, or you are also calling them dirty, stupid, slaves, etc. This is why nowadays most forms that request for one's racial status, no longer reads 'Black, White, Coloured, Indian, etc.' but it reads, 'African, White, Coloured, Indian, etc.' Society has accepted the lie that Black is not Beautiful; a lie generated by many years of bastardizing our culture and Black people. The worst that Apartheid did wasn't to oppress black people but to destroy their unique sense of humanity. In a class system, 'Black has been associated with the lower classes. In other words, if there is a choice between a 'suburb' and a 'township'; an excellent school and a poor-performing school; a beautiful mall/park and an unmaintained mall/park, the option where the conditions are worst will automatically be associated with Black people, and the option where the conditions are best with White people – this kind of perception is not only made possible by Whites against Blacks; but Blacks themselves perceive each other this way; this is how they see their Blackness. This way, consciously or unconsciously, they have come to identify themselves with slavery and the conditions thereof. This leads to a situation where nobody wants to be Black or be associated with Blackness. This is okay for other races, but it is problematic for the black community; it leads black people to a

situation where they don't want to be them-
"selves"; where they are so ashamed of their
Blackness that they somehow manage to
convince their subconscious mind that
they're not Black or that they're a different
kind of Black people. They have no sense of
responsibility toward their Humanity to
live out and perpetuate the African
heritage; so deep is the idea of 'not being
Black' entrenched in their subconscious
mind that they gain a sense of "self" by
deviating from the African culture and
language. They no longer perceive
themselves as being Black; but as
individuals with Black skins. There's a vast
difference between the two:

Being Black refers to proudly modeling the
African way of life, in as far as it is
possible, through your daily speech, your

actions, your fashion sense, etc. it refers to being an embodiment of Blackness and being completely comfortable and proud of the state of your Blackness. Being an individual in a Black skin means that you just have Black skin, but your essence has nothing to do with Blackness. The problem is that these "individuals in Black skins" move away from Blackness toward adopting other cultures and lifestyles which are not Black. Modernity and capitalism have both assisted in creating this kind of a Black person – where the stress is on the individual, the "I" and not the collective, the "we." The irony about this kind of Black is that he believes that he's modeling his 'own way of life' – which is rarely possible. When you live in a Society, your character, values, perception, etc. is part of what that

Society has made it to become because from birth, you were introduced to 'Convention', and you were inculcated with the ideas thereof. By this, I mean, you were taught what certain words mean, how certain letters and numbers look like, how a chair looks like, how the colour blue looks, who GOD is, etc. You didn't just spontaneously come into the world and introduce your own ideas about GOD; start writing a book in your own self-created language etc. – then you would be a very isolated individual. You can do so later in life, but it will always be within the confinements of what you've been taught; how you've been taught to perceive. Equally, one can't just create their own, absolute new way of life; it will always be within the confinements of how they've been taught or influenced by others to perceive Life. So usually, these individuals in Black skins never really create their own, unique way of life; they just deviate from the African way of life toward another way of life – usually a Western-influenced way of life; just like Black Western celebrities or the majority of black youth in South Africa. These individuals in Black skins are lost; without a heritage; without a true humanity.

Many people will disagree and say that they don't associate Blackness with slavery and the conditions thereof; I have met such people. On one occasion, I asked one of them, a young Black woman named Thuli, what she would do if she saw a white garden boy. This is how the dialogue went:

Me: So Thuli, what would you do if you saw

a white garden boy?

Thuli: Well, I wouldn't do anything, but I'd feel satisfied; I'd feel that it's "right!"

Me: But...doesn't the very fact that you react that way suggest that this experience is not normal to you?

(She nodded)

Me: ...it indicates that it's not yet normal for you to perceive the Whiteman as a garden boy. You would feel satisfied because you're not used to the idea. Your mind will find it more normal to perceive the Blackman as a garden boy, but slightly weird to perceive the white man as one.

Our minds have been conditioned by historical events to associate White-ness with excellence and Black-ness with slavery and the conditions thereof. This is understandable considering the many years that Black people have been exposed to slavery and the many years that White people were exposed to ill-gotten privilege; however, that doesn't excuse it as a state of Unconsciousness. In order for Black people to progress in what Steve Biko calls, "their quest for a true humanity", this kind of mind conditioning has to be eliminated. Firstly, it is not true; it is a result of the psychological bastardisation that the Apartheid system intended to inflict on the Blackman. And secondly, it is the greatest enemy to Black people's "quest for true humanity": It is a fact that can't be brushed off that South Africa, as well as the rest of the world, still needs to get used to the idea that the black community has "realized" themselves as a people. That the black community is equal to any other community, and as much as it is normal for the Blackman to be a garden boy, so it is normal for the white man to become a garden boy; as much as it is normal for the White man to become a CEO of a large corporation, so it is normal for the Blackman to become a CEO of a large corporation. Black people haven't yet claimed their rightful place in global politics and economics, where they can, as a people, firmly say their share and influence the direction of global politics and economics. For them to move toward such, they first need to develop a strong sense of their own humanity, where they can see themselves as being more significant than the white man, if not equal to him – they need to learn to be arrogant, in a sense, but also maintain the modesty and humility that is their African Heritage. This may seem like a contradiction, but it is actually not. By arrogant, I mean that they must be able to lay a firm stake regarding the direction of global politics and economics without being 'puppeteered' or influenced by Western countries in any way. They have to stop compromising their culture and heritage for the sake of world peace but instead demand that world peace be adjusted to exist within their culture and heritage. They need to be able to make the United Nations see things through an African people's lens, instead of Africans always having to see things through a European/Western lens. This is the kind of arrogance I refer to – the arrogance that will help give the world a more African face. This can be achieved with modesty and humility. This is not an arrogance that seeks to dominate the world; it is an arrogance that tries to make the world realize the humanity of the Blackman – that he is also an equal global player. This will help eliminate the idea and global perception that Black is not Beautiful.

Society has become so sensitive to race-politics that if you include the issue of colour anywhere, you are deemed to either be racist or as trying to create a sense of separation between Man. The fact is, a part of humanity's history was primordially based upon colour and in order to overstand and explain current social trends in behaviour, perception, etc. one must inevitably include the issue of colour. The means to bring about unity in our global society shouldn't be about trying to ignore colour, cultural and language differences and trying to create a homogeneous society; but it should be about realizing these differences and creating a global environment in which each difference can exist and be recognized equally, so as to embrace the beauty of Man's diversity. It should be about trying to put a heterogeneous society into one bowl, where we are all on the same ship and can Love and Appreciate one another on the grounds of our shared humanity. By trying to create homogeneity, we are insulting the Intelligence that made us diverse. This is actually the only way that we CAN live; it is either this, or the whole world will soon have a Western face. According to Dr Joel Freeman's work, Table of the Nations, there are only basically three races: Africans, Semites and Whites; however, I want us to look here at the skin aspect of these three race-categories, with language, heritage, location being negligible. When one reads into Dr Joel Freeman's work thoroughly, one overstand that what he's actually implying by these three race-categories is that there are people with brown skins; people with white or pink skins and people whose skins are a blend of the two – and these he qualifies as Semites, although he includes more than just Jews or Arabs. By Africans, he basically refers to everyone with brown skin, and by Whites to everyone with a white/pink skin; however, by Semites, he refers not only to Jews and

Arabs but all other people with similar skin colour. These would be the Portuguese, Asians, Chinese, Brazilians, and Indians, etc.

This differs slightly from the apartheid ideology: The apartheid ideology only perceived Whites and Non-whites, and the non-whites were basically seen as being Black. When one spoke of 'Black people, ' one was essentially referring to Africans, Indians, and Coloureds. It was a spectrum from white to non-white, and in that spectrum, everything that is white was beautiful, and as you move along the spectrum, the more non-white you are the less beautiful you were. Black-ness was bastardized. So bastardized in the minds of Society that to be associated with it is almost a taboo, to the extent that people gain a sense of "self" from the idea that they're not Black – such as many whites, Indians, and Coloureds do. The 'Black' labeling has now automatically been associated with Black people; it is too late to refuse it or resist it; it is ours, now perceived to be part of who we are. However, there is nothing wrong with Blackness; there is everything wrong with the way society perceives it. Blackness has been so associated with slavery and the conditions thereof much that Black people because they are Black, have come to think that they are slave-like or a lesser people – and this has further been supported by the general attitude of Society itself toward Blackness. However, in this kind of situation, Blackness needs to realize that it no longer matters how Society perceives

Blackness, but how we perceive it, which will dictate the way we will model it to the rest of the world. If Blacks start believing that Black is Beautiful and proudly live out their Blackness, then Society will realize how wrong it is, and they will begin to be influenced to perceive Blackness as being beautiful. No one is going to help Africa realize her beauty; she has to do it all by herself.

'Skin' Colour

Apartheid thinking still manifests itself subtly in our education system and English language thereof. In primary school, we are taught the different type of colours, and there's one colour which we are taught to identify as "skin" colour type. And it is no coincidence that this colour is one that resembles the skin colour of white people. In other words, from an early age, our children are taught to refer to white skins as "skin" colour, and brown skins are merely called brown. Isn't brown also skin colour? This example bluntly manifests the arrogance of white people. It is clear that this kind of device is meant to subliminally establish white people as more human than Black people in the young learner's mind. All that relates to white people is made to look and sound good and respectable, and the more non-white you are, the worse and less worthy things are. It is not that it's the way things are; it is that it's the way white people want them and made them be. Using every opportunity, they can to prove their supposed falsified and well-marketed superiority as a people. That can be easily changed and should be changed if we want to move toward a united, democratic South Africa where everyone's humanity is truly respected. Firstly, the colour called "skin" colour in our schools shall be called "skin" colour no more; we shall call it light peach; that colour which is called "nude" in your cosmetic kits shall be called "nude" no more; we shall call it light peach. Not because that's what we want, but that's simply how the colour looks: It doesn't look like skin, nor does it look nude; it looks peach. Black people primarily suffer from Unconsciousness in the same way that white people people suffers from an Ego: A constant, pressing need to establish themselves as a superior people. They roll up their windows when they see a Blackman walking past their car on the sidewalk, they clutch their handbags when a Blackman walks behind them in a mall, they feel uncomfortable in a neighborhood when Black people start moving in. They have fixated specific ideas in their minds about Black people that make the Blackman an 'inferior being' in their eyes, and that makes them superior. "Black people are thieves, Black people are noisy and filthy, Black people are poor," etc. They make Black people "wrong" so they can feel "right"; they make Black people "small" so they can feel "big" – whether consciously or unconsciously. When they are kind toward Black people, many of them do it from a place of contempt. This seems to be the only way that they can gain a sense of self. This is the disease that white people largely suffer from – the Ego.

The Apartheid system helped feed the belief that the white man is inherently superior and better off than the Blackman simply because he's white. The quest to prove this is actually that triggered apartheid in the first place. Why couldn't they come to South Africa and allow both societies, Black and white, to develop separately and independently? Why the need to oppress another People? Why couldn't they do what Black people did for them? Allow both Blacks and whites the opportunity to live and develop themselves freely? Post-1994 Black people didn't call for the oppression of the white man; they only called for an opportunity to live and develop themselves freely – that was enough. This could suggest that they believe they can be naturally great and equal to the white man without manufacturing an oppressive system that would be in their favour as Apartheid was in the white man's favour.

It is not that white people today are wealthier and smarter; it is that they manufactured an Apartheid system that gave them an exclusive advantage to be that way. When Black people won their freedom, they didn't take away the things white people had accumulated, instead they said, "It's fine, let them keep what they have and let us even not hinder them from acquiring more; as long as we now also have the chance to accumulate these things, we shall accumulate them for ourselves and by ourselves." This is indeed a noble act.

So let us not live in a South Africa where we try to prove that one society is better than the other; that Blacks are better than whites or vice versa. For if some of you still think this way, there are many things about Black people that make them better than white people, in as much as there are many things about white people that make them better than Black people – and the two cancel each other out. We are all human, and most importantly, we are all South Africans. If only Black people can accept their current collective state of Unconsciousness, and if only white people can recognize their current Egoistic state, then both would be liberated, and we would move on to create a beautiful South Africa.

In this section, let's begin with the first step: Start calling what seems light peach, light peach; not "skin" colour or "nude" in cosmetic/make-up kits.

African Nationalism and the expression of Blackness

In understanding the concept of Black/African Nationalism in South Africa, it is necessary to partake into the genealogy of the philosophical outlook by drawing from the likes of Tiyo Soga, Solomon Plaatjie, Anton Lembede, AP Mda, Robert Sobukwe Steve Biko, and so forth and so on.

And although the ANCYL (African National Congress Youth League) has previously served as the nucleus for African Nationalism in South Africa as early as the 1940s by championing the concept and cause of Africanism which asserts that, in order to advance the struggle for freedom, Africans must first turn inward and reflect extensively by shedding their feelings of inferiority and redefining their self-image, rely on their own resources, unite and mobilize as a national group around their own leaders; one would argue that we are mentioning the Youth League simply because these earliest ministers of African Nationalism in Post Tiyo Soga and Sol Plaatjie – Anton Lembede, AP Mda, Robert Sobukwe were preliminarily a part of the ANCYL until they left the Movement in

1959 to form the Pan African Congress (PAC) and by then, Anton Lembede, a sentimental figure in the expression of this remedying ideology was no more, after his earlier death in 1947 due to alleged natural causes. However, on its manifestations in present-day thought leadership development, it would be immaterial to subordinate the idea/spiritual basis of Africanism to neither the ANC or the PAC or any political party for that matter because Politics have only served the dispersing doctrine of divide and conquer since the 1994 elections. On the other hand, the ANC's practice of Colourblind politics of equality resurfacing on non-racialism and non-sexism sloganeering without addressing the injustices brough front by Apartheid and Colonization in South Africa after 342 years only serves the opposite of what African Nationalism seeks to accomplish. Non-racialism or rainbow nation without reparatory justice has only left black people subservient under the plague of white supremacy because the origins of contemporary suffrage today can be traced back to the racially disenfranchising 1990-1993 CODESA negotiations where everything took place. Black leaders and reformers could only argue for political inclusion on the grounds that only persuaded liberal or moderate whites that nothing revolutionary or contrary to generally accepted political norms were being proposed. This was also evident as PW Botha, in 1987, after a meeting with Nelson Mandela advised that he was not in a position to meet with anyone with revolutionary ideals, henceforth subconsciously exposing a political figure Nelson Mandela was becoming. All those compromises came at a great price. Prominent political figures like Chris Hani were assassinated in the process and many other unknown figures whose deaths might not be explained for atleast another 100 years and we cannot ignore that part of our reality and a country's history today. So, because of the compromises, the current status quo promotes a racially divisive society where blacks are on the bottom whilst comprising 90% of the country's population and White people on top with a population below 10%. And the status quo is the order of the day today without a radical reproach to addressing the injustices of the past than "epoch-making statements" without deliberate commitment to serving black people by the African National Congress government.

Towards the end of overt white racism in the late 1980s, the number of rights to which humans were normatively entitled would increase partly as a result of black protestors, orators, thought leaders, and writer's efforts. But the struggle for a conception of human rights that would outlaw all forms of racism is still a long and frustrating one. Above all, the ANC have also adopted Neo-liberalism or liberal equality whereas liberal equality means an equal right to acquire and protect private property rights and the ANC is living to see the realization of the promises they have made between 1990-1993 with the latter patently evident today with many events proving this supposed belief, eg. protestors were killed in Marikana by black Policemen, who as part of protecting private property rights above Human Rights have mass murdered about 34 miners and injured hundreds.

As we fast forward to the country's democratic era, black people today cannot even go to supposed professional environments without suffering demonization because of the blackness of their Skin. The schooling system is even worse, our children can't even wear their Afros and locks because it's unprofessional – they must relax/straighten their natural hair to be considered more acceptable and professional which brings us to a conversation around what blackness means as previously understood by those who came before us. Some believe that Blackness is not skin colour or biology; rather a social definition. They argue, that It is possible to look "white" physically and black socially just like Steve Biko and the BCM coined Black as a mental attitude and as a result created a hybrid political definition where Indians were also regarded as blacks instead of Asiatic, but I stand to defy this analogy in defense of biological, cultural and genetic history.

Now talking about expressing blackness. Let's first be clear about something. When White settlers came to Africa on a mission to conquer, own, control the continent, whatever they couldn't own, control or conquer like the Blackness of our skin – they demonized. They stole our arts and sciences, our inventions, our spirituality, our history and civilization, and everything else that came with all of that. So, anything that they could not make theirs terrified them much they destroyed and demonized those. This includes the Blackness of our skin; hence they killed, raped, sold, molested, dehumanized, oppressed, and repressed us. And that is why they cannot stand our hair hence in schools and corporations, Dreadlocks and Afros are regarded as unethical and unprofessional and that right there is the demonization of our blackness.

They demonize Black people's hair because our hair represents our strength; it forms an antenna through which the spiritual force may descend. Hair is the receiver and transmitter of divine intervention, -it makes you receptive to spiritual forces, and it helps embrace, revitalizes and activate your Pineal gland henceforth oxidizing the Melanin biochemical, therefore, reproducing biochemical substances and Spiritual frequencies that produce and reproduces themselves. So, by discouraging black people, particularly black women to hate themselves, that's spiritual castration. When black women begin to wear other races' hair, their point of entry (Natural hair) to the spiritual world gets lost. And you can now see women on social media saying they are having a bad hair day when on their kinky hair. So, to express blackness, you need to have a thurely knowledge of self because it is impossible to express something that you do not know of. Whites have demystified blackness much that when we think black, we think savages, death, drug dealers, criminals, inferiority, etc.

My thoughts on the Blackman

First, I think the Blackman, particularly in South Africa has been successfully domesticated - spiritually, materially, economically, socially and if ignored, may become a useful instrument in the mass extermination against Black people which has already started in time immemorial:

• There is a mass raping of Black women and, in most cases, as a consequence,

Murder/genocide by the Blackman.

• There is a mass robbery of Black victims by mostly, Black men,

• There are countless cases of the Kidnapping of Black Victims, by mostly black men,

• There are countless cases of human trafficking and forced Prostitution of Black Victims, by mostly Black men and amongst many other social ills, contributing to the self-negation, self-hatred and the self-destruction of Black people.

In Post-Apartheid South Africa, we can see the Blackman a symbol used to destroy himself, the black woman, and black babies but how is that possible? Given the ambitious and genetic orientation of men; as part of their biology - asserting one's ego is deeply embedded in our DNA, which in most cases - it happens to be the assertion of Material resources, in which, the absence of such material resources may lead into the disposition of that energy - self-condemnation, self-hate, self-negation and self-destruction; hence we see a whole lot of psychologically displaced black men participating in the aforementioned drastically. Also, thus we see black men, in the absence of material resources (Land, Wealth and family) they end up asserting their Masculinity by bringing other Black men and Black women down, boasting about your Levi's, Range Rovers, Louis Vinton, and other immaterial assets that got nothing to do with the Black community. Proposed Remedy: It is crucial to understand the creative Genius that colonization was; this was to displace, dehumanize, economically deprive and hold black people to the level of mere objects; hence we are today the greatest opposer of the Fourth Industrial Revolution, because our value is only comparable to objects in society - to serve. 1. Now, to reverse this misdemeanor; we need the psychological reorientation of the Blackman, being the basic weapon used against the self-destruction of the black race, 2. When the dehumanization is reversed, the most significant economic boycott against White economic institutions is necessary and where possible, an industrial revolution and a complete destruction of White economic institutions, 3. Re-writing the Blackman and the Black woman's memory in order to regain our family hypothesis which was the central part of also, our spirituality. While Black men and Black women are physically extant to have families, they are spiritually isolated and must be reunited. 4. Build communities, including our economies and institutions of learning. With Love and peace, from your brother!

What is the Black inferiority complex?

For the longest time now, especially within Black Consciousness and Black Nationalist circles, we have endorsed the interpretation of Black people's embrace of their denigration as The Black Inferiority Complex since Anton Lembede and Steven Bantu Biko. So I would like to cross-examine this modeling as we retrospect on our fast-growing investigative Consciousness towards Black Intellectual thought as time calls for the evolution of the latter.

It would be incorrect for us to embrace "concepts," Cosmology-s, Typology-s, Ontology-s, and epistemology-s if we don't really know what they mean in Scientific literature. Blackness, according to traditional African societies, is a spiritual constituency. This means our Melanin, Our hair, our eyes, lips, skin colour forms part of our essential cultural makeup. And our history, spiritual systems, Cosmology-s, Typology-s, Philosophies helps elevate our way of life and our mathematical calendar if indeed the purpose of mathematics is to complement our art and sciences. So, with the topic at hand, it's essential to establish what the concept/noun Complex means so that our isolated response towards black submission is adequately understood. The word complex's dictionary meaning is; Consisting of so many different parts and elements. So will that not mean that the Black inferiority complex is self-explanatory? In the Black inferiority complex, we have many different parts and elements that have been put together to develop an identity of inferiority in Black people, namely; 1. Religion, 2. Spiritual Castration, 3. Land dispossession, 4. Scientific Racism (Law of Evolution), 5. Economic extermination, 6. Psychological Collapse, 7. Social destitution etc.

So in favour of the concept, we should put together means to deal with the Inferiority complex; because the complex is not a sentiment that can be addressed to those whom we trust suffers from the former - it is a well-established system, so as we continue to experience its repositories within our black brothers and sisters' psyche, we should instead try to help them out attentively so because they are subconsciously participating in their demise.

Chapter 6

<hr/>

White arrogance in Contemporary times

*S*outh Africa is the very last country to gain independence out of the 54 African States. Our colonization lasted for over 342 years since Jan Van

Riebeek's invasion in 1652 until Nelson Mandela's democracy in 1994. For more than three decades, black people exclusively caught hell from white people. Like I had already said, the first institution that Dutch settlers built when they arrived in 1652 was the prison. So bear in mind, to this very day, prison is a power dynamic reinforcing mass incarceration in an era of subtle but more definite structural racism.

They enslaved, dehumanized, raped, and systematically domesticated all Bantus in South Africa; the Khoisan, the Xhosas, the Zulus, The Sothos, The Tsongas, The Vendas, The Ndebeles, the Swatis, etc. Although today they distort the history of a people. They continue to creatively assert that they have only dispossessed the land from the Khoisan as if Khoisans are not blacks, and this is because they have recently socially engineered a new Khoisan breed with their verminous blood in them so that they can claim this country by instrumentalizing colored brothers and sisters. Any coloured who think Khoisans are not black is not a Khoisan descendant, to begin with, and if they are – the system has successfully domesticated them. Any White person who thinks Khoisans are not black should equally go to hell. Overhead I shared a quote from Penny Sparrow, a white racist who denoted that black people are monkeys, and this was in January 2016, 22 years after Mandela's democracy. This continued mockery and contempt of black people by whites is proof that South Africa could only have reached a compromise for democracy provided that black people are being compromised, because white people continue to systematically castigate black people through institutionalized racism and economic discrimination using institutions such as banks etc.

The economy is still in the hands of whites, the land in the hands of whites, the country in the hands of whites; the factories, industries, media, and the privilege are all bestowed in white hands. So it is rather impartial for me to acknowledge the fact that black people have been successfully domesticated; hence we continue to catch hell from the same enemy. Penny Sparrow referred to black people as Monkeys. The very same blacks who have forgiven three hundred and forty-two years of Genocide, but still, we forgave all that hell we have wedged from White people through explicit racism and White terror domination, and today, we are nothing but a comic show in the eyes of white people - it's a shame. Again, another incident happened in 2017. Democratic Alliance leader Helen Zille Tweeted that "For those claiming the legacy of colonialism was only negative, think of our independent judiciary, transport infrastructure, piped water, etc." Then again – it's a shame. The Apartheid system didn't only systematically miseducate black people to embrace the idea of inferiority compared to whites, but has also dehumanized white people to embrace the idea of supremacy compared to blacks. Colonialism was very bad, and if she is one of these many White supremacists and nationalists who believe that Africa was a jungle, before European colonialism and black people were singing and dancing with monkeys, then she has been thinking wrong. In this regard, that's where you realize that Charles Devil (Darwin)'s theory of Evolution or origin of spaces was very purposeful, and whites, on the other side, have too, been successfully domesticated. So we are both scientific projects of White racism. The only difference being – Whites were prostituted into superiority, and Black people were castigated to inferiority.

Black people civilized the world, and any white person who believes the opposite is only like us - a victim of psychological abuse. Whites understood the importance of knowledge and information; hence they systematically destroyed the existence of black civilization on paper to theoretically propose a discourse that was to become an adopted "original History" taught in schools now — a psychological crime! So it's troubling to realize that the reconciliatory project was compromised because this signifies that Black people sincerely gave out their sympathy in anticipation of the same in return from whites, and not only have we been wrong — we were cheated. The symbolic sympathy from whites should have come in the form of reparations — repairing the colonialism and Apartheid harm. In the absence of reparatory justice, atleast big corporations and banks were supposed to be taxed for reparations — reparations tax. And also, black employees working for big white corporations would then need to benefit to some degree from different subsidies – housing and property acquisition and business capital. But all that never happened. Instead, the racism is subtle, but more prominent now than it has ever been in recent history.

Today, the land is significantly and economically viable enough to enrich all citizens – but the African National Congress has signed suicide deals during the Convention for a Democratic South Africa (CODESA), and there is no going back. Mining remains privatized and out of all state-owned resources – the Mining sector is the most significant national treasure, but they are not in charge of the same. The De Beers, diamond miner, owned by Anglo American, controls our overall diamond production, circulation, and distribution in South Africa. In contrast, the same company is having a different arrangement in Botswana and Namibia. In Botswana, they mine in a consolidated venture with the Botswana government's Debswana with a 50/50 profit share. Again in Namibia, the same company mines in a consolidated joint venture with the Namibian government's Namdeb Holdings, equally with a 50/50 profit share which is direct evidence of how nationalization can be manifested without the expatriation of preceding diamond gangsters but in a regulated system of Government control but here in South Africa, the same De Beers company is privatizing the Diamond mining business with no profit share with Mandela's ANC government and they, in addition, pay their black employees close to nothing. So how can we be respected by

White people when we continue to serve under their terms? The 1994 negotiation compromise is not apprehensible because blacks were compromised, for which was nothing new. After all, we have been compromised for more than three decades to the extent that a Genocide was launched on us, and the Truth and Reconciliation Commission was imposed on black people under the guise of Rainbowism and whites remain the "Baas." The year 2016 was a fascinating period in my life, a year to remember. I was blessed with my first born-child − a beautiful princess in her right. But most importantly − I received a lot of revelations. Although there is just one specific revelation, I would like to share. This came in the form of a dream (a very long one). I had a dream in what may seemingly be understood as racial profiling against Whites when overlooked. In the dream, there was an assembly of about 15 or 16 White males. All of them wearing "Khakhi Shorts" and seated, when one of them stood up and had the following to say (Seemed like the Willie Lynch letter, I could have displaced some of the contents, but this is what I could still recall as I wrote everything down as I woke up):

"My white brothers, we have given the Blackman politics, but a good part of this is that we still have our forefather's land, we still control the economy that we have built for so many years and also, we have his mind right where we need it. The media system has played a pivotal role in this, which is excellent – so let's keep up the excellent work (everybody claps). As for the Bantu education, also, on that front, we have not been doing bad although the blacks are waking up, something needs to be done consistently and as a matter of urgency. So since we still have our diamond, Gold, Platinum coal mines, and more, we need to ensure that we retain as many minerals as we can in this land of blessings, the land of our forefathers. In contrast, we still have the time, and most importantly, we must preserve the minerals more than to mistakenly overproduce to the maximum, if needs it be, let's maximize on our labour force and production – to the extent that we can clean all the natural resources if possible because these blacks will someday wake up. Let's also try, by all means, to downgrade their capacity to make end means for our benefit, and for the heritage of the most powerful generation to come in a thousand years from now so that our great Grandchildren can continue to rule over the Blackman even when we are six feet under (A few laughs) and black people should serve them as they have served our forefathers, us and our children.

So we have a few issues that we need to resolve first before we can celebrate our God-given Supremacy against these Monkeys;

1.   Let's convince them to believe that they cannot survive without us (In this case, Zimbabwe's situational analysis gives us much reference and must be weaponized against their thinking) - Fear conquers all battles, so what we need to do now is to spark fear in black people and threaten their very survival in the absence of Whites in Africa. How do we do that? Let's continue to write them books (We have been doing well in that front), convince them that before we came to Africa, they were singing and dancing with monkeys. Make strategic movies about their history to convince them further of who they were in the past and control their entire narrative of self. And

that way, if we can convince them that we civilized that when all they were doing was hunting and dancing, they will, therefore, see nothing wrong with our systematic perpetuation of economic domination and will not question our superior status because they will for which they already do - believe that we have improved their human condition. Don't allow them to talk about Ancient African Civilisation; because we will have a problem and a massive one. If they can know about such a history, they will, in turn want to be in charge of their concept of self, that way, they will not need us and they will henceforth eat us alive. Let's try and profile Ancient African history as conspiracy theories so that we can continue to lead, and they can continue to serve. We are their leaders, are we not? (everyone laughs).

2.   Let's continue to control the schooling and labour systems – let's control their working hours, and by all means, try to

manage the times they spend bonding with one another. Let's ensure that the Black male and the female adult goes to work from morning to night and make sure that the young Black kids spend more time in school and when back from school, they should do homework so that by the time they think of organizing late in the evening, they are already tired and will then need to sleep and focus only on waking up earlier. I promise you that way when the weekend comes, they will focus on relaxation or going out with the family to have fun, and they can't have time to organize. I can see that you are curious, but let me break it down for you my fellow supreme beings for you to understand much clearly (Everyone nods):

Let's plan down their lives - Let's make sure that from birth, they will go to school at the age of six, so the best we can do is increase the number of schooling years to twelve and above, but then if it's twelve years, also consider that some will be failing in the process. So to ensure that the majority fails a couple of times, we need to create a very complicated syllabus and keep changing it per year. We should ensure that the minister of education is a black person; that way they can blame one another – guess who wins? Us (they all clap). So if the person never failed a class, the expected finishing year is age 18. Now, after matric, let's have them go to university for four years to obtain a degree/Diploma (and since we already control private University, this is an added economic advantage), so after four years, they would be 22. Therefore, we should point out the fact that they don't have experience for the applied job and offer them learnerships where they will do the actual work, but as learners in the company's books, that should last for at least one year at a very minimum wage. By then, they would be approximately 23. After a learnership, take them as interns, a year-long in a minimum wage. After then, they would be 24. Therefore after that, we can then employ them and pay an average salary, which can only help them earn a living. Consequently, we must ensure that we supply their employment information to all our stakeholders (Banks, etc.) so that we can offer them "loans", "Houses on bonds that can only be payable in Twenty years" so that they can work on the job for Twenty years more to finish paying the house. So after Twenty years, they would be 44 with limited Industrial opportunities, and they would be bound to work for eternity and serve us. Such a desperate Black is a worthy slave to keep because they are desperate.

3. Let's control and manipulate their concept of self and the world - For the fact that the rising Consciousness of these monkeys just cultivates out of nothing all the time. Let's project them monkeys as

criminals, Thieves, drug dealers, and help them kill each other, and let's create chaos out of them. And how do we do that? Let me break it down for you.

3.1   Let's sell them alcohol and arrest them for getting drunk, and for ensuring that many of them drink as much as possible, we must make adverting beer an essential daily. Let's produce movies where victims use beer to soothe their frustrations so that when they are in similar positions, for which is daily to them, they will escape to alcohol. We will find an excuse to arrest them and call out campaigns against substance abuse and portray blacks as those who drink a lot, but we should make sure they don't take the substance abuse campaign to beer factories.

3.2   Let's create drugs and arrest them for selling and also for using it. Let the world perceive drug dealers as the worst and must ensure that that the majority of these drug dealers are black savages; you distribute these drugs to black sellers much that even our children buy it from them so that we can accuse them (these monkeys) of corrupting the world and therefore, use the police force to shoot at them at times. The people will be unconsciously celebrating this and will start running campaigns like "Stop drugs abuse," whereas we know that we are the ones who make the drug, but the campaign will have nothing to do with us (clap in laughter). But take their mind much that they don't realize who the enemy is (Smiles).

3.3   Let's make guns and produce television content where owning a gun and shooting at people is random; envisages content that makes them think that going to jail is fun, and they will in turn shoot and rob each other and go to jail, and therefore, we will have ample time to profile them as criminals.

3.4   Let's distract them through social media (Our own Facebook, WhatsApp, Instagram, Twitter) so that they can spend much time on their phones and not bond together. Let us manipulate the natural process of humanity so that they can be comfortable and not pay much attention to Land, their inheritance, their history, their society, and above all - everything that we have stolen. And when they try to use social media, again, let's distract them. Let's come random news stories that exist (Black people love jokes, and they will start making memes) and not focus on things that may see our future no longer possible in this continent. We also need to make sure that black people fight amongst themselves and their black politicians. Let the Zulus fight with Xhosa's, The Tsongas fight with the Tswanas, The pedis with the Vendas, the Ndebeles with the Xhosa's, the Swatis with the Sothos, etc. Let them have much-increasing hatred amongst one another so that we remain the only unifiers.

Because I warn you, my white brothers, that our survival in this continent is dependant on the ignorance of these Apes. When you see them, please smile at them each time so that they can become comfortable around white people – this is called symbolic psychological manipulation. When they talk about race relations, please mock their content and tell them to stop living in the past, and that way, they will accuse each other of hatred when one of them talks about their truthful and painful history – for which I believe it was well deserved, where would we be?

4. Let's win the heart of the black woman - Let's understand supreme beings that the strength of these criminals lies in their females. So this is what we do. Let's start empowering the black woman and accuse the Blackman of being the reason behind the black woman's delayed progress.

Let's tell the black woman how evil the Blackman is. He rapes her, he abuses her, treats her like an object, and we must put her in a permanent state of agitation against her Blackman so that unity amongst them is impossible; that way - the black woman will be on our side. Let's break the two's bond by coining the term feminism for the female, and patriarchy for the male, which means that the Black woman should stand for herself since the black male has failed her. Let's taint the Blackman's image in the eyes of the black woman so that she can see no reason to have such a man, and we can start empowering the black woman much that she becomes financially secure as compared to her black male – he must be weakened.

When all of that is done, let's find more innovative ways to keep distracting the black race, and we will rule them until the end of the world. (The end of the dream).

I had this dream, and I was scared for days, I thought maybe those were results of thinking hard about systematic exploitation while at the same time, when I analyzed the dream in-depth, everything made sense based on what's happening. I remember when I woke up that very day around 1 am, everything felt so real, and I had to write down everything as I remembered, and I stayed woke until the dawn of a new day. Everything around me felt so strange for days, and I must admit that the dream is what triggered me to write this very book. I know it may sound prejudicial to white people, but I can't help it. I value truth because when I grow up, I used to lie about everything.

Chapter 7

Thoughts During Corona
Virus' Lockdown and the
Politics in South Africa

The year 2020 marks a hundred years since the Spanish flue of 1918-1920 that killed over fifty million people globally. Ever since then, there has never been a comparable pandemic of that magnitude.

As we began this year, no one would have thought that by May 2020, we would be dealing with the Lockdown catastrophe amidst a median economic collapse. As such, there are many differing views regarding on whether or not the virus exist and I'm on the of the people who are critical on the existence of the Virus, and if whether or not it is an act of God.

THE NOVEL CORONA VIRUS OTHERWISE ACRONYMED COVID-19 IS A GLOBAL SCAM, AND IT'S SCIENTIFICALLY IMPOSSIBLE FOR IT TO EXIST

If anything is revealing in 2020, and possibly in the past Twenty-six years since the African National Congress took over from the rebellious and racist Regime of

Apartheid Mafias after four hundred years, is this Global Paradox so-called Corona Virus or Covid-19 disguised as a Pandemic - a very hegemonic discrepancy. Unlike other pandemics like cancer, having killed nine million people in 2017 only, without any Lockdown nor restrictions, Corona Virus is a Hogwash and likely, don't even exist. Science relies on evidence to prove a hypothesis, but you will be stunned to realize that the Corona Virus Hypothesis, having been popularized by:

1. The World Health Organization in conjunction with Wuhan, China,

2.Billionaires and the pharmaceutical industry,

3. Governments,

4. The Media

Haven't been scientifically proven and justified, but here we are. The system manipulates our lives; the median economy is shutting down, and the new world order is in progress whilst your president, Cyril Ramaphosa and a few opposition leaders like your Mosioua Lekota, Julius Malema and others are butt licking and butt dancing towards billionaires and top pharmaceutical companies, and ordinary people carry the burden of such pettiness. There is no time for book clubbing and singing amid a mid-time scam: this is the time to do some "Act-clubbing" and some swinging. On top of that, as if singing is not enough, your opposition is even singing for an extension whilst enjoying the luxuries of a stay at home in their middle-class mansions, notwithstanding the anguish we have undergone under this myth-making period in our lifetime.

If Corona Virus exists without Bio-transmission as a biological weapon, what are the causes? And don't tell me how it's transmitted and so forth, but I need the causes. They say that the symptoms of Corona Virus, which they argue is a respiratory infection, include; fever, difficulty with breathing, a low immune system, also, people with an existing chronic condition or weakened immune system are the most vulnerable. So does this mean this is an opportunistic disease? But what is an opportunistic infection? Except it's a biological weapon typically created in some lab for Population control. What if their testing kits form part of the bio-transmission? And the vaccines that are likely to be imposed against our will? What they refer to as symptoms of the Corona Virus are actually symptoms of the Upper body respiratory Infection.

What are the symptoms of the upper body respiratory infection, and how is it transmitted?

" An upper respiratory infection, or the common cold, is an infection that affects the nasal passages and throat. Treatment is usually simple, unless a person also has a chronic respiratory condition such as asthma. For an upper respiratory infection (URI) to occur, a virus enters the body, usually through the mouth or nose. A person may transmit it through touch, or by sneezing and coughing. Any place where people gather in an enclosed space, such as a classroom, office, or home, can be a high-risk area for the spread of URIs." [https://www.medicalnewstoday.com/articles/323886]

So, in this case, what's new about the Corona Virus except for Human population control and inscribing the New world order to control Humanity while profiting tons of billions in US Dollars in the process. On top of the fear that they have been circulating through News reporting and propaganda machinery we are mandated to wear a Face mask, whilst breathing in and out the same Carbon di-oxide which then maximizes the chances of brain damage and breathing difficulty, which will make possible the biological weapon to be infested in your system.

We cannot be controlled and silenced by the Political elite in partnership with the Pharmaceutical Mafias and World.

SOUTH AFRICA IS HEADING TOWARDS COMPLETE RECOLONIZATION IN THE NAME COVID-19, AND ALL CITIZENS ARE SUBCONSCIOUSLY PARTICIPATING BY ACCEPTING THE R350 BRIBE

The year 2020 has marked yet another critical period in Human History, a phantom of terror masquerading as the Covid-19 Pandemic. Exactly about a hundred years ago, another pandemic relative to this experience between 1918-1920 in the form of Spanish flu had hit the world harder than no other in recent history. The global response to the Spanish

Flu pandemic was not so different from what's currently happening in the world. Schools were closed; businesses were closed, people's movements were restricted, etc. But regardless, it is estimated that the virus affected over 500 million people globally, with about 17-50 million recorded deaths. So it is such an incredible coincidence that a hundred years later, a similar event is taking place – but this time around, a lot is happening in the world. As much as Covid-19 has already been declared a global Pandemic, it is still subject to further scientific scrutiny; to determine whether it is fortuitous or a well planned biological weapon since to date, there have been reports that some of the so-called Corona deaths are ipsa facto not even a result of the Corona Virus. For example, if anyone was to die of Malaria, even in their death ward, if they were to be diagnosed with Corona, such a death would be recorded as a Corona death case. On her peak of recovery in the fight against Corona, China has released a report that some of her recovered patients still tested positive and henceforth reprimanded the testing kits as faulty (A very critical aspersion worthy of investigation). And in the interest of truth, here in South Africa, on the 27th of March 2020, a report was released by the Government that a 28-year-old had died of Corona Virus. Still, a few hours later, the Health Minister, Zweli Mkhize, re-issued another statement that the 28-year old didn't really die of Corona Virus. With this in mind, it is henceforth necessary to interrogate the statistics surrounding Corona Virus cases; most countries like the USA and China believe that some of the testing kits are not 100% reliable, so a possibility of false positives could also be at play. But why would the whole world pursue a thrust in numbers for Covid-19 cases? Could this be leading towards mandatory vaccines and population control?

In South Africa, the response towards the Corona Virus pandemic has been extreme, particularly with the Law enforcement's position during this period – radical domestication of black people. The first precision towards the Lockdown took place as of 26 March 2020. And despite the underlying factors surrounding lockdown restrictions, one couldn't help it but notice the legacy of Apartheid and Colonialism in

South Africa during this period. As much as the restrictions were "allegedly" for the best, the majority of black people staying in areas without running water, proper sanitation, Skwatta camps, etc. had to suffer the most, more than what the Pandemic itself could have done. It is clear that if you have no running water on your yard, you will need to grapple with a wheelbarrow to the nearest tap, or if you can only afford a loaf of bread per day, you will need to at least buy two loaves to last you for about two days henceforth making random trips to the store or for whatever reasons there is out there. It is clear that during Phase 5 of Lockdown, people were not openly disregarding the Lockdown for the sake of so doing, particularly the majority of suffering people. Our circumstances are much more deadly than Covid-19. And our ill-trained soldiers' response towards the former has been nothing but the torture of the most vulnerable people in South African Society today. To date, about nine people, black people, have been killed by the South African National Defense Force (SANDF), and the President hasn't said anything yet regardless of the many press briefings he has had. But since we have the power of social media these days, we have witnessed the circulation of pictures and videos of police forcing people to do frog jumps and push-ups – our Mothers, Fathers, sisters, brothers, and cousins; and most likely, this happens to be black people. In an event where a white citizen is concerned, some amount of respect was given during the

Lockdown period – This is exactly what the Apartheid government promoted through its police and security forces; The social degradation of black humanity. So how is Cyril Ramaphosa different from Hendrick Verwood?

On Tuesday, 23 April 2020, when expected to confirm the opening of the South African economy and the lifting of Lockdown restrictions, Cyril Ramaphosa instead advised that the country would be opened on a phase-to-phase basis upon which we were to move from 5 with the most harsh restrictions to phase 4 with still harsh restrictions but a few exceptions. Most importantly, a significant concern in all of this is that Cyril Ramaphosa ran to the International Monetary Fund to raise the R500 billion budget to fight against

Covid-19. However, the IMF is notorious for taking over so many country's economies with its binding loans. In his transaction of South Africa, Cyril has employed a very critical ploy, bribing every citizen with a R350 cooldrink – so that tomorrow he can openly say that he didn't eat or drink alone – he ate with everyone. But also, about the R350 cooldrink/bribery, that amount itself is ridicule to the value attached to the citizens of this country. The United States of America, of course, a superpower has issued a fund relief of $1200 (R20 000) for every US citizen, Nigeria about R2500, Botswana, about R750 amongst others who tried by all means to give a relief fund that indeed helps during Lockdown; otherwise, the R350 in South Africa is just bribery. It shouldn't even be issued because it perpetuates an unnecessary liability that relieves nothing but cost us our beloved country. The ANC government, under the leadership of Ramaphosa, is making it clear that South Africa is now a Police State, a direct result of Apartheid in South Africa since they have released an extra 70 000 soldiers by April 2020. Why are they not making a concerted effort toward the intensification of health facilities if this indeed is about the Corona Virus?